An
Empowered
Witness

An Empowered Witness

Sermons and Writings of Paul S. Rees

Edited by
Glenn D. Black

Beacon Hill Press of Kansas City
Kansas City, Missouri

Copyright 1997
by Beacon Hill Press of Kansas City

ISBN 083-411-660X

Printed in the
United States of America

Cover Design: Mike Walsh
Cover Photo: Westlight

Library of Congress Cataloging-in-Publication Data

Rees, Paul S. (Paul Stromberg)
   An empowered witness : sermons and writings of Paul S. Rees /
edited by Glenn D. Black.
      p. cm.
   ISBN 0-8341-1660-X (pbk.)
   1. Sermons, American.   I. Black, Glenn D.   II. Title.
BV4253.R39   1997
252' .0995—dc21   97-8967
                                               CIP

10   9   8   7   6   5   4   3   2   1

CONTENTS

Paul Stromberg Rees
(1900-1991)

Foreword

The appearance of a real preacher is remarkably like an unusual sunrise. It is obviously a work of God. The preacher brings with him light like dawn so that darkness flees. Even the hidden crannies of life are illuminated. Spiritual coldness retreats and warmth spreads everywhere. Hard hearts melt and joy dispels our gloom. Common folks rejoice and say that God has visited His people again. The prophet understood this:

> How beautiful on the mountains are the feet of those who bring good news, who proclaim peace, who bring good tidings, who proclaim salvation, who say to Zion, "Your God reigns!" (Isa. 52:7, NIV)

That is the way it was with Paul Rees. He was a preacher. He was a pastor, a writer, an evangelist, and a missionary statesman. Preeminently, though, Paul Rees was a preacher. Wherever he went (and he went almost everywhere), the light of the gospel, with its warmth and illumination, went also. There was a clarity and a winsomeness in the presentation and an artistry that befitted the message.

It is good to know that, within the pages of *An Empowered Witness*, some of Paul Rees' work is being made available again. For those who never heard Dr. Rees it will not be quite as good as for those who can remember the lilt and cadence of his voice. But then that is what those who heard and knew Jesus would say about the Gospels, isn't it?

This material is good enough that I trust a host of us who try to preach will carefully study the message and the method. If we do, I am sure there will be more who will rise up and call us, as well as the publisher, blessed.

—*Dennis F. Kinlaw*

ACKNOWLEDGMENT

Special acknowledgment and thanks are due the B. L. Fisher Library of Asbury Theological Seminary for permission to reprint the sermons and writings of Paul S. Rees that appear in this book. The rights to these materials are held by Asbury Theological Seminary at the bequest of Dr. Rees.

INTRODUCTION

Paul Stromberg Rees was born September 4, 1900, in Providence, Rhode Island, to well-known Holiness Quaker evangelist and preacher Seth Cook Rees and his wife, Frida Marie Stromberg Rees.

At age 17 Paul Rees announced his call to preach. He delivered his first sermon at a downtown skid row mission in Los Angeles. After graduation from the University of Southern California in 1923 with a bachelor of arts degree, he emerged from that humble scenario and became superintendent-pastor of the Detroit Holiness Tabernacle (1928-32) and was senior pastor of the First Evangelical Covenant Church in Minneapolis from 1938 to 1958. He addressed congregations, pastors, ministers, and students in more than 60 countries. He delivered his final sermon on Easter Sunday morning in 1991 in Boca Raton, Florida—more than 73 years after sharing his first one. He traveled by train and car thousands of miles during the early years of his ministry and an estimated 7 million miles by airplane during his illustrious preaching career.

Beginning his ministry within the shadows of a very eloquent and powerful preacher father, Paul Rees was soon recognized by his peers as preeminently an expositor of the Word who had the rare gift of combining simplicity with the profound, thus making an appeal to both the child and the scholar. It is noteworthy that as he interlocked his work with the preaching career of his father, whose own ministry spanned the period of 1874 to 1933, the Rees father-son ministry team harvested spiritual fruit from 1874 to 1991—117 years of preaching and ministry!

In a personal letter written to me on May 7, 1991—13 days before his death—Dr. Rees requested "a place of remembrance" in my prayers. Suffering from a collapsed vertebra, he told me that the Lord had given him "peace in the midst of pain." He added, "At the same time, He has kept alive the fire that burns for the communication of His Holy Word." What a declaration and passion after 73 years of preaching!

Paul Rees was one of the towering Evangelical leaders of 20th-century preaching and writing. He authored 14 books and wrote columns in the *Asbury Herald* (1961-75), *Covenant Companion* (1959-72), and *World Vision Magazine* (1964-72). His biblical understanding, his spiritual maturity, his intellectual strength, and his homiletical skills set him apart from the ordinary preacher and writer.

Billy Graham stated in the late 1960s, "Few men speak as well as Dr. Rees. But he has achieved the rare gift of writing as well. His personality comes through in every paragraph and leaves people reaching for new heights of Christian living. He jabs the conscience and challenges the mind. Yet in his speaking and writing, the love of Christ comes through clearly, leaving no harshness. Few men are so adept at metaphor, illustration, and picturesque speech." A. W. Tozer once said of him, "If Paul Rees were to split an infinitive or flub a single word in his preaching, the cosmos would collapse."

Paul Rees was a servant of God and His Church. Richard Halverson, recently retired chaplain of the United States Senate, said, "If Paul Rees taught me one thing, he taught me the lesson of servanthood. Paul taught me that I'm a servant to servants for the Servant."

Paul Rees revered the Bible. He truly worshiped Christ. He was a convinced advocate of Christian holiness. He was sure of his vocation. He loved his family. He served the Church. He had an incredible love for his fellow preachers. He was a consumer of truth and not merely a connoisseur of theological terms. Such convictions as these gave his soul the "surge of the sea" and his ministry the "strength of the oak."

Paul Rees died May 20, 1991, the way he lived—prepared.

The contents of this book include three sermons (noted as "sermon classics") selected from the hundreds of manuscripts he left. They represent his theological thrust. The other printed materials are condensed and edited sermons and writings from the heart and mind of Paul Stromberg Rees—a 20th-century Christian statesman who speaks articulately to the 21st century.

—GLENN D. BLACK
DISTRICT SUPERINTENDENT,
KENTUCKY DISTRICT
THE WESLEYAN CHURCH

PART I

Basic Recognitions

1

IF GOD BE FOR US!

A Sermon Classic

"IF GOD BE FOR US, WHO CAN BE AGAINST US?" (Rom. 8:31).

This is the great challenge that Paul set on its sturdy feet and sent marching down the far from easy path of the Christian centuries. I wish, by heaven's help, to set it ringing in our ears and in our hearts as, vaguely conscious of the weakness we represent in ourselves, we put our humanly feeble feet on the threshold of a new year.

"If God be for us, who can be against us?" With these terms does a bold Christian confidence gird itself. It rises, all rugged and splendid, out of the midst of a great marshaling of majestic truth; for the eighth chapter of Romans marks one of the highest levels of revelation in all this Book of God. As someone has pointed out, it begins with "no condemnation" and ends with "no separation"! The last 14 of its 39 verses constitute the immediate setting of the text; and, with them as a background, let us examine this thrillingly triumphant word.

Let us, however, remark in a general way on the contrast that is here declared: for and against! Explain it as we may, deny it we cannot, there is a dualism in life from which it is impossible to escape. A moral cleavage cuts its keen and uncoverable way straight through the universe. There are things that are for us, and there are things that are against us. And these things, according to the inspired conception of the apostle Paul, not only group themselves, not only exist in conflicting confederacy, but, traced up to their sources, are found to be centralized and personalized. Our text names the One, the high and holy One, who gathers up unto himself and presides over the things that are leagued for goodness and for all who seriously purpose goodness for themselves. And while it does not name him, the text does, by the use of the personal pronoun, suggest the personalization of evil, whether the opposition be human or satanic.

But the point is that the contest is not an equal one. God is almighty; Satan is not. Wickedness may make more noise, but righteousness can muster greater strength. Life's insurrectionary and destructive forces are formidable, yes, devastating—let no one be so stupid as to deny their reality or their vitality—but they are no match for the redemptive and healing energies released from the broken heart of God on the mount called Calvary. Show me the man or woman who aligns himself or herself with God, takes a bold stand there, makes unconditional surrender there, and I will show you a man or woman who is so divinely environed, so linked with Omnipotence, as to secure for himself or herself the restful assurance of final everlasting triumph. Swing that person from the gibbet, burn him or her at the stake, grind him or her to powder, and before you are done with your thankless task, the vaulted skies will ring with that believer's victory shout, flung full-throated from the battlements of glory: "Thanks be unto God, which always causeth us to triumph in Christ" (2 Cor. 2:14).

"If God be for us, who can be against us?"

Now an attempt to interpret these words in the line of thought of which they are a part will lead us to consider that

1. *God is for us ELECTIVELY in the purposes of His grace.*

That is the point of verse 29, which reads: "For whom he did foreknow, he also did predestinate to be conformed to the image of his Son, that he might be the firstborn among many brethren."

Thus in a vast stretch of thought are we carried back to mystic beginnings, back of Calvary with its shadows and anguish, back of Bethlehem with its cradle song, back of Sinai with its thunder-toned pronouncements of law, back of the Garden of Eden with its sinless symphony of physical beauty and moral purity, back of creation's wonder chorus when the morning stars sang together and the sons of God shouted for joy—back, back, back, where, in the counsels of the infinite Mind and Heart, the story of man and woman got its start. Even there and then we—you and I—were given a place in the eternal purpose of God.

Well aware am I that this is treading ground strewn with the weapons and scalps of many a theological gladiator. Not for a moment does one presume to offer any final word on the mystery of how the divine foreknowledge and foreordination are to be reconciled with human freedom and human responsibility. He or she who speaks too glibly or dogmatically here commits the folly of rushing in where angels fear to tread. But of one thing we may be very sure—it is an unshakable conviction born of an effort to hold a balanced view of the teachings of God's Word—and that is that if a person is saved, it is by the grace of God, and if a person is lost, it is by his or her own refusal of the offer of that grace. Any view of the doctrine of election that arbitrarily limits the atonement of our Lord Jesus Christ, or that arbitrarily elevates certain individuals to eternal life while it consigns certain others to eternal death, can be held only by eyes blind to the fact that God wills not the death of any, but rather "that all should come to repentance" (2 Pet. 3:9).

When a candidate for the ministry told John McNeil that he was perturbed with the thought that he might sometime offer free grace to one who was not of the elect, the noted Edinburgh preacher is reported to have answered, "Oh, mon, don't let that bother ye. If ye should happen to get the wrong mon saved, God will forgive ye." Thus it is that betimes a bit of humor happily rescues us from the peril of extremes to which we seem driven by the rigor and vigor of our often too-cold theologies.

In taking leave of this thought of God's eternal purpose of grace, there are two suggestions that one would lift into prominence. First, you, my friend, and you have a place in that purpose. You are dear to God. You mean something to Him. You are even now the subject of influences and the object of planning, the origin of which is older than proud Egypt's pyramids and finds its home in the heart of the eternal Father. The second suggestion is that the blessedness to which you are elected in the filling of your place in His purpose is nothing short of holiness, or Christlikeness. I use the words synonymously because the Scriptures do. The same Holy Spirit who declares in the context, "Whom he did foreknow, he also did predestinate to be conformed to the image of his Son" (Rom. 8:29), declares in Eph. 1:4 that "he hath chosen us in him before the foundation of the world, that we should be holy and without blame before him in love." There is a large sense in which Christlikeness must ever remain merely an approximation with us; but there is a proper sense in which it can be, by the grace of God, an actual, living realization. Christ was holy and without *fault*—there is your approximation. We can be holy and without blame—there is your realization. A heart cleansed from all sin by the precious blood of Christ is a heart whose moral texture of motive and purpose is inwoven with the mind of Christ.

And this suggests the second proposition to which our study brings us:

2. *God is for us EFFICACIOUSLY in the cross of His Son.*

The question of the text is followed by another question. "If God be for us, who can be against us?" Then the apostle seems to say in effect, "Do you doubt that He is for you? If you do, answer this further question: 'He that spared not his own Son, but delivered him up for us all, how shall he not with him also freely give us all things?' [Rom. 8:32]."

What God has purposed in eternity He provided for in time in the incarnation and atonement of the Lord Jesus Christ. Let us not be confused by the clamor of contradictory voices heard on every hand. The delivering up of Jesus, His vicarious sacrifice upon the Cross, is the central fact in the whole revelation and realization of God's redemptive purpose. To it all preceding ages point the way; from it all succeeding ages take their rise. The Cross effectively removes those barriers in the divine nature that would prevent a holy God from making cheap concessions to sin, and it effectively produces the highest type of moral appeal to morally responsive beings, inciting them, as nothing else has ever done, to a hatred of sin and a love of righteousness.

Ah, yes, He was delivered up for us all! And since He was, says Paul, shall not the Father God give us all things—such things, for example, as the luminous chapter unveils?

Shall He not forgive us our sins? Answer: "Whom he called, them he also justified" (Rom 8:30). "Therefore being justified by faith, we have peace with God through our Lord Jesus Christ" (5:1).

Shall He not confer upon us, who are by nature aliens and by choice rebels, the title of sons, sons of God? Answer: "Ye have received the Spirit of adoption, whereby we cry, Abba, Father. The Spirit itself beareth witness with our spirit, that we are the children of God" (8:15-16).

And having forgiven us our transgressions, having put upon us the benediction of His pardoning peace, shall He not deliver us from our carnal-mindedness, from the subtle enmity of self-will and self-love? Answer: "For the law of the Spirit of life in Christ Jesus hath made me free from the law of sin and death" (v. 2). The *life* of sinning is one thing; the *law* of sinning is another thing. The life of willful sinning ceases at conversion, but victory and freedom as touching the law of sin in our moral nature is the glorious privilege of God's children who will be filled with His sanctifying Spirit.

Shall He not, moreover, teach us the secret of that mysterious ministry that we call prayer, that something by which, as Tennyson put it, more things are wrought than this world dreams of? Answer: "Likewise the Spirit also helpeth our infirmities: for we know not what we should pray for as we ought: but the Spirit itself maketh intercession for us with groanings which cannot be uttered" (v. 26).

And would not time fail us to tell of *all* those divine ministries and human benefits that flow down to us in an endless stream from the crimson fountainhead at Calvary? God went the limit at "the old rugged Cross." He gave us His best. And that "best" is the red banner we lift in confidence that "no good thing will he withhold from them that walk uprightly" (Ps. 84:11).

3. *God is for us ENCOURAGINGLY in the mysteries of His providence.*

Blessedly familiar are the pertinent words of the 28th verse: "And we know that all things work together for good to them that love God, to them who are the called according to his purpose." Mark the certainty of it—"we know"! That is characteristically the language of Christian conviction. But do not fail to mark the limitation of it: "to them that love God, to them who are the called according to his purpose." To *them* the immense pledge is given; concerning *them* the inclusive declaration is made, that "all things work together for good."

I stood one day with a friend in a salon of Marshall Field's in Chicago, where magnificent tapestries were on display. In front of us was one whose rare beauty of design and marvelous skill in execution made it particularly impressive. Curious about its cost, I stepped over and turned up the corner to see if I could find a price mark. I found it—$6,000. But I found something else. I made the discovery that this expensive tapestry had two sides, and that if Marshall Field's had hung it up wrong side out, it would not have brought $6, to say nothing of $6,000. That back side was utterly without design. Threads ran crazily in this direction and that. It all looked like the work of a nitwit. Yet those were the very threads that, worked by the masterly hand of the artist, had produced the exquisite picture that appeared on the other side.

Have you put your life into the hands of the infinite Artist? Have you really? Then have the faith and courage to believe that, however strangely the threads may seem to run, however cruelly the needle may stab you, it is His hand at work—and back of His hand His heart.

Then, changing the figure, let this be your steadfast stand:

I will not doubt, though all my ships at sea
Come drifting home with broken masts and sails;
I will believe the Hand that never fails,
From seeming evil worketh good for me.
And though I weep because those sails are tattered,
Still will I cry, while my best hopes lie shattered:
"I trust in Thee."

I will not doubt, though sorrows fall like rain,
And troubles swarm like bees about a hive;
I will believe the heights for which I strive

Are only reached by anguish and by pain;
And though I groan and writhe beneath my crosses,
I yet shall see through my severest losses
The greater gain.

I will not doubt. Well anchored in this faith,
Like some staunch ship, my soul braves every gale;
So strong its courage that it will not quail
To breast the mighty unknown sea of death.
Oh, may I cry, though body parts with spirit,
"I do not doubt," so listening worlds may hear it,
With my last breath.

—Ella Wheeler Wilcox

It can be done by those who abide in the confidence that "all things work together for good to them that love God."

But we have not yet reached the climax of the discourse out of which the text speaks so significantly: "If God be for us, who can be against us?" For us *electively* in the purposes of His grace, for us *efficaciously* in the cross of His Son, for us *encouragingly* in the mysteries of His providence, the apostle now reveals Him as the One who will be for us forever.

4. *God is for us ETERNALLY in the fellowship of His love.*

"Who shall separate us from the love of Christ?" (Rom. 8:35) is the daring defiance that Paul lifts against all comers. He feels himself in the warm embrace of the love that will not let him go, a love that now whispers and now sings of the life of love that is to be "unmeasured by the flight of years," a love for which he counts all things but loss and holds life itself as a consecrated forfeit to that infinite affection.

This is no cheap faith we hold and preach, this Pauline, this Christian faith—no puppy love transferred to the realm of the religious. Here is a love bond that nothing but sin can break, not "tribulation, or distress, or persecution, or famine, or nakedness, or peril, or sword" (v. 35). "In all these things we are more than conquerors through him that loved us. For I am persuaded, that neither death, nor life, nor angels, nor principalities, nor powers, nor things present, nor things to come, nor height, nor depth, nor any other creature, shall be able to separate us from the love of God, which is in Christ Jesus our Lord" (vv. 37-39).

The evidence is in. The argument is finished. God is for us—has been for us through the eternity that stretches back of us, wants to be for us throughout the eternity that rolls ahead of us. There is but one point unsettled. And what is that?

In a critical hour in the American Civil War a somewhat fearful individual exclaimed to United States President Abraham Lincoln: "Oh, Mr. President, I am most anxious that the Lord shall be on our side!"

Back came the Lincoln reply, characteristically terse and penetrating: "Well, strangely enough, that gives me no anxiety at all. The thing that I worry about is to make sure that *I* am on *the Lord's* side!"

And therein lies the point! The divine position has been taken and announced. What shall ours be? Who is on the Lord's side? That is the supreme question of the hour. I appeal to you: answer it aright. Take your stand with Him, that you too may lift your confident challenge: "If God be for us, who can be against us?"

2

When Repentance Is Real

More than 15 years after World War II, the moderator of Japan's United Church of Christ journeyed to Korea to address a large assembly of Korean Christians. He said, "I would like to apologize to you on behalf of all the Christians in Japan for the countless evil doings that our government and people committed against your people. . . . I hope you will be pleased to have this assurance of our repentance. . . . I beg you on behalf of my people and in the name of our Lord that you will forgive us."

This reminds us of something the apostle Paul once wrote to the Corinthians: "Godly sorrow worketh repentance to salvation not to be repented of: but the sorrow of the world worketh death" (2 Cor. 7:10).

Note that Paul is referring to people *all* of whom, he assumes, are exercised about the guilt feelings that possess them. Some, he declares, are going to miss a complete cure; others are going to find it. The difference is that in one case the repentance is not real, adequate, Christian; in the other case it is.

There are three ways to tell when repentance is real.

To begin with, repentance becomes, in the Christian sense, effective when it *goes beyond the feeling of subjective grief and truly faces up to God.*

Elsewhere Paul speaks of the gospel that he preached as consisting of "repentance toward God, and faith toward our Lord Jesus Christ" (Acts 20:21). Repentance toward God! That, I believe, is what the apostle means in our text by "godly sorrow." The sense of shame is there, to be sure, but it concerns itself with something more than the emotion we feel or the consequences we face for our wrongdoing: it concerns itself with the staggering fact that we are *what* we are and *where* we are because we have left God out of our lives. We were meant for God, and God was meant for us. And we have spoiled the pattern.

Furthermore, repentance, to be genuine, must *pass beyond sorrow to surrender.* Paul makes it plain that the heart of Christian penitence is not reached until we move beyond the emotion of sorrow. He declares that "godly sorrow worketh repentance." The conviction of sin and the shame of it must lead to *action.* It must be the spur to a high and Christ-enabled decision of the soul.

There is that unforgettable prodigal son, of whom the Master told us, in the far country. His money has been spent, his friends have taken leave of him, his fine clothes are in rags, his proud spirit is broken. His menial and filthy job is to look after the pigs, which, since he is a Jew, he loathes. Now, at length, he is thoroughly ashamed. He burns with self-reproach and disgust. But that would not have spelled repentance.

He goes farther. "I have sinned," he bitterly confesses. Even that is not enough. Then comes the moment and the act in which there stands revealed the core of Christian repentance. He deliberately, sincerely, decisively announces, "I will arise and go to my father" (Luke 15:18). Jesus adds, "He arose, and came to his father" (v. 20). And *that* is real repentance. True repentance is not to be measured so much by the violence of our emotions as it is by the sincerity of our surrender.

One more word! Repentance, to be real, must *pass beyond failure to faith.* We now return to the reminder Paul gives us in a passage already quoted from Acts 20:21. The apostle sums up his gospel in a double statement: "repentance toward God, and faith toward our Lord Jesus Christ."

For all who are now oppressed with a sense of guilt and shame, for all who are ready to make this an hour of decision, this is the key question: Will you have faith in God and His Word?

God is trustable. Yet we treat Him with fear and hesitation. We are like the boy who once appealed to Mr. Sam Hadley as the greatheart of the Bowery sat outside the Water Street Mission in New York. The little fellow asked for a piece of cloth and a needle and thread. He wanted, he said, to mend his trousers. Hadley looked him over. The ragged clothes seemed scarcely worth mending. Suddenly the chap began crying. He had stolen $20 from his father in Philadelphia and run off to New York. "I've spent all the money," said he, "and I'm afraid to go home."

"Go back," said Hadley, "and your father will take you in."

"No, he won't," said the boy, and nothing could convince him otherwise.

So off went a note from Sam Hadley to the father: "Dear Sir: Your boy is very, very sorry for his sins. He is in my mission here and wants to come home. What shall I tell him?"

Before the next noon a telegram was in Hadley's hand: "Tell the dear boy he is forgiven and I want him to come home at once."

Jesus assures us that God is like that. Swifter than any telegram, more dependable than a government bond, comes this word to us now: "If we confess our sins, he is faithful and just to forgive us our sins, and to cleanse us from all unrighteousness" (1 John 1:9).

3

Spirit of Burning, Come!

OF THE MANY DESCRIPTIVE PHRASES used in Holy Scripture to identify the Spirit of God, one of the most vivid and arresting is given us by Isaiah. The prophet speaks of "the spirit of burning" (4:4). True, the Authorized Version uses "spirit" without capitalization, but numerous scholars and commentators have assured us that we are not wrong in thinking of this as a reference to the Holy Spirit.

Nor dare the Church of Christ ever forget that on the Day of Pentecost it was "cloven tongues like as of fire" (Acts 2:3) that becomes a symbol of the searching, purifying, illuminating ministry of the Spirit of God.

And when, years later, Paul would warn the Christians against the sin of choking off the vitalities and the spontaneities of the Lord, who by His Spirit lives within them, he said, as Phillips renders it, "Never damp the fire of the Spirit" (1 Thess. 5:19).

Let's remember that there is a *burning out* that is of the Holy Spirit. Isaiah, as his first chapter makes clear, had heard the Lord God say to His covenant people, "I will . . . purely purge away thy dross" (v. 25). Five chapters later he gives us a dramatic account of his own experience of passing through the fire of God's cleansing; "Woe is me! for I am undone; because I am a man of unclean lips" (6:5). The confession was the prelude to the cleansing. His lips were touched, he tells us, with "a live coal" (v. 6) from the altar of God, and the assurance was given him, "Thine iniquity is taken away, and thy sin purged" (v. 7).

Are there not within many of us unworthy values that need to be burned out—values too chaffy and cheap to rate continuance in the life of anyone who means to put the kingdom of God first?

Are there not low motives that need to be burned out?

"All meanness," cried dear Samuel Zwemer in one of his sermons, "all hatred, all envy, all impurity, all criticism, all suspicion, all jealousy, that is in your heart or mine will disappear if we just throw it into the crucible of Christ's loving soul." The day he said it, he was preaching on the Holy Spirit as the fire of Christ in the soul of human beings.

Furthermore, there is a *burning in* that is of the Holy Spirit. The burning out of the litter of the unholy is never an end in itself. The aim and end of the Holy Spirit's fiery work is the burning in of Christlikeness. Recall Paul's word to the Corinthians: "But we all ['all of us who are Christians,' as the Phillips translation puts it], with open face beholding as in a glass the glory of the Lord, are changed into the same image from glory to glory, even as by the Spirit of the Lord" (2 Cor. 3:18).

Years ago I was guided through the famous Rookwood Pottery in Cincinnati. I saw vases worth hundreds of dollars for which certain lovely designs had been prepared. These vases, with nothing on them but painted patterns, would never have brought a high price. But they went into a furnace. They were subjected to intense heat. The pattern of beauty was burned in. The resulting enhancement was permanent.

A keen young Christian helped a drunk from the gutter, called a taxi, and got him home. When they parted, a sobered gentleman said to his young benefactor, "If Jesus Christ ever lived on earth, He must have been like you!"

It is not our relationship to Christ—which in a sense is known only to God—that is important in witnessing; it is our resemblance to Christ. And that is not our achievement. It is the work of the Holy Spirit. It is by the burning in of the Master's image.

Finally, let's face it: there is a *burning up* that is of the Holy Spirit. The writer to the Hebrews, in an extraordinary piece of phrasing, tells that our Lord "through the eternal Spirit offered himself without spot to God" (9:14). While the supreme climax of that offering was at the Cross, His whole life was a sacrificial outpouring. That is to say, it was by the Spirit that the continuous burning up of dedicated energies, gladly expended for the glory of the Father and the saving of men and women, happened.

Under normal conditions fire means three things: ignition, combustion, illumination. Without ignition there will be no fire at all. But also, without combustion there will be no illumination. The combustion is the burning up of fuel and the giving forth of energy and light.

In any field of endeavor look for the people who are on fire and going places. When you find them, you will discover that they are people who do not spare themselves, coddle themselves, withhold themselves. Their life energies are the fuel on which the fire of their purposes feeds.

It is not different in Christian living and creative spiritual service. Life must be given, yielded up, unsparingly—one is tempted to say recklessly—if the Holy Spirit is to make full use of Christ's man or Christ's woman as a healing, guiding light in the kingdom of God.

Never can I forget the impression first made on me many years ago when, standing beside the grave of Methodism's famous scholar-saint Adam Clarke in City Road, London, I read the simple epitaph: "IN GIVING LIGHT TO OTHERS I AM BURNED AWAY."

4

SATAN THE SIFTER

THE BIBLE, FROM GENESIS TO REVELATION, takes for granted the reality and subtlety of the devil. Jesus spoke of him freely and solemnly—and let no one say this was merely His way of accommodating himself to the folklore of the times.

"Satan" means *opponent, destroyer.* God is harmony, but there is a devilish discord everywhere in His world. God is beauty, but there is a devilish ugliness that disfigures man's character in high places and low. God is constructive, redemptive, but there is a devilish destructiveness that blights and ruins.

Let us consider Jesus in conversation with His friend Peter. More than three years had passed since Peter ceased being one of Satan's allies and became, instead, one of his registers. Had Satan given up, reckoning Peter permanently lost to his cause? Not at all! And because Peter was too little aware of this, the Master plainly puts him on guard: "Simon, Simon, I tell you that Satan has obtained permission to have all of you to sift as wheat is sifted" (Luke 22:31, WEYMOUTH).

Satan's tempting activities are somehow permitted by God. There is mystery in this—and some people are badly stumbled by it—but the fact is there nonetheless. God has created us as moral beings who are temptable. He has, moreover, allowed Satan and his evil agents to be the instruments through which these solicitations to wrong come to us.

Since Peter is singled out for special warning by our Lord, I suggest we try to think through three angles Jesus could have had in mind when He issued this solemn warning about "Satan the Sifter."

For one thing, this man Peter illustrates how dangerous Satan can be when we are under *criticism*. Recall the day when Simon Peter came, ruffled, I suspect, and said to Jesus, "Lord, how oft shall my brother sin against me, and I forgive him?" (Matt. 18:21). And then, not waiting for the Master's reply, and thinking of that person who had made life miserable for him, picking at him, finding fault with him, Peter added in a strained attempt at magnanimity, "Seven times?" (ibid.).

Seven times! That sounded bighearted and patient and forgiving enough. So Peter fancied. What a jolt he got when the Master said, "Until seventy times seven" (v. 22)!

It is not so much the Savior's reply that concerns us here; it is the nettled apostle's query. I think we are entitled to gather that Peter was even then in Satan's sieve. The edges of his soul were getting raw, for they had been raked by criticism. It was precisely the hour for bitterness to form within, for resentment to become a rancid deposit in the soul.

Whether you and I are criticized justly or unjustly is not of first importance. What is really important is the way we react to the criticism. If we are reacting with resentment or censoriousness, we are in Satan's sifter. Unless we face this in honesty and renounce it in sincerity, no release from it will be ours by the power of the Spirit of God.

Move along now to another realm in which Satan tries deftly to get us into his destructive sieve. If he cannot get us through the criticisms we undergo, he will attempt it through a *confidence* in which we rest. Peter's was a misplaced confidence, and it nearly wrecked him completely.

In the Mark account of this conversation (Phillips translation) we hear Jesus say, "Every one of you will lose your faith in me." But Peter protests, "Even if everyone should lose his faith, I never will" (Mark 14:27, 29).

"'Believe me, Peter,' returned Jesus, 'this very night before the cock crows twice, you will disown me three times.' But Peter protested violently, 'Even if it means dying with you, I will never disown you!'" (vv. 30-31, PHILLIPS).

Great swelling words, you see, springing from a great swelling self-confidence! But the balloon is soon pricked. The gleam of self-assurance gives way to the burning blush of shame.

Think for a moment about the foolish self-confidence of professing Christians who, having met their Lord in a deep hour of being utterly surrendered to Him and filled with His Spirit, will get right into Satan's sifter the moment they begin to rest in the *experience* instead of resting in the *indwelling* Lord. It is dangerous to suppose that the longer we continue in victory, the safer we are.

I appeal to you, Christians: never put confidence in the length of time you have been a believer. Never put confidence in the past triumphs of life. There is but one place of safety—in the faithful Lord who, living within you, expects nothing of *you* but failure, while you expect nothing of *Him* but victory—His victory made yours!

The *criticisms* we undergo, the *confidence* in which we rest, and then the *companionships* in which we walk: here too Satan sets up his sifter. In John's account of Peter's denial of his Lord, we are given a vivid picture of the apostle in bad company. In the courtyard of the high priest's palace, where they had taken Jesus to bring false charges against Him, they had built a fire for comfort in the chill of the night. "They were . . . warming themselves; Peter also was with them, standing and warming himself" (18:18, RSV).

Was he there to help these people understand who Jesus was? Not at all. And in that atmosphere, where he stood warming himself at the devil's fire, he made a mess of his testimony and a shambles of his discipleship.

If you value your Christian faith and your Christian character at all, have a care about your friendships. If you run habitually with the godless, God will become unreal to you. If you run with the lazy and the shiftless, ambition will wither in you.

Are your friendships helping you understand Jesus Christ better? Are they stimulating and challenging you to make more out of prayer and to think more about the eternal qualities of life?

If not, then I tell you plainly you are in Satan's sifter. When he has finished with you, the wheat will be gone. The chaff, and the chaff only, will remain. Satan the sifter! How tirelessly he works!

Listen quietly, please, as I remind you that our Lord's *warning* word was followed by His *winsome* word in the context: "Simon, Simon, behold, Satan hath desired to have you, that he may sift you as wheat: but I have prayed for thee, that thy faith fail not: and when thou art converted ['when you have turned back to me,' as the Phillips translation puts it], strengthen thy brethren" (Luke 22:31-32).

If you are in the temptation stage of Satan's sifting, my warning is for your awakening. If it has gone beyond that, and you are in the stage where there has been yielding to temptation, where defeat has planted its black flag within your soul, and you know it, my exhortation is for your encouragement. A pitiable Peter, with the curses of hot denial on his lips, was broken in shame and penitence by one unutterably compassionate look from Jesus. And Peter was restored.

Even as you can be!

5

WHY CHRIST
MAKES SENSE

THE TELEPHONE RANG ON A MONDAY MORNING. A lady was speaking. She said immediately that she wished to withhold her name and then described a situation that had suddenly confronted her in her own home. It shocked and outraged her. Her question to me was "What would you have done in a situation like that?"

Notice the significance of the word "done." "What would you have *done?*" Jesus said, "Whosoever heareth these sayings of mine, and *doeth* them, I will liken him unto a wise man, which built his house upon a rock" (Matt. 7:24, emphasis added).

Whatever else life is—including, most emphatically, the life of the Christian—it is eventually a matter of *practice*. It is a way of *behavior*.

Something else is suggested by that woman's earnest, almost desperate, inquiry. The question, "What would you have done?" implies *choice*. One must choose between two or more ways of behavior.

In any case, our telephone conversation soon brought out the fact that whatever we might decide was the best thing to do would be determined by our *standards*, or *ideals*. She reminded me that some parents, upon discovering what their children were doing, would have experienced neither shock nor distress. I had to acknowledge that she spoke the truth. But why would such parents react so differently, so unconcernedly? Might it not be that their standards were different? Therefore their judgment of the matter would be different.

Now all this is a springboard from which we take our first leap in this discussion, namely, that behind *Christian behavior* we must have *Christian standards*. That is, we must have some fixed principles by which we test the rightness or wrongness of our practices.

Jesus, for example, raised up and strengthened an old standard when He declared, "Therefore all things whatsoever ye would that men should do to you, do ye even so to them" (Matt. 7:12).

Christian conduct, says Jesus, as it relates to the treatment of others, requires that we try to put ourselves in the other person's place. If wrong is being done, obviously we cannot approve it. We cannot condone it. We cannot lightly tolerate it.

On the other hand, if we have regard for the Golden Rule, we cannot engage in sheer condemnation. We cannot be satisfied only to deal out a penalty (unless perchance all redemptive means of meeting the situation have been exhausted).

For it must not be forgotten that in the Christian scheme of conduct there is not only justice but also grace.

These are considerations this mother would need to have taken into account if she wanted to put into practice the *Christian* principles that have been sealed and signed by our Lord Jesus Christ.

So far, then, we have simply made the point that conduct is related to standards. We must now press the matter further.

If conduct is tied to standards, standards are tied to values. Since we are sitting at the feet of Jesus, let it be said at once that *Christian standards* depend upon *Christian values.*

In the broad sense, values are of many kinds and degrees. They are "goods," whether material or nonmaterial, that are believed to have worth. The lower values are those that fall into the class of means, as in the case of money, which we do not value so much for what it is as for what it will *purchase.*

The higher values are those that fall into the classification of ends; that is, they have worth in *themselves.* Music, for example, is clearly of higher value than money. We prize music because it offers that which is inherently satisfying and worthful.

Our Lord recognized this pattern or system of values. Look at those sparrows, He said one day in the midst of His teaching. They have value, but it isn't great. As for you, said Jesus as He looked at His disciples, "Ye are of more value than many sparrows" (Matt. 10:31).

We need to be struck with the full force of that personal pronoun—"ye." Here Jesus drives home to us the unique value of men, women, boys, and girls as persons. A person differs, not slightly, but vastly, from *things* and from *animals.* He or she possesses self-consciousness—the ability to choose, to say yes or no to optional forms of behavior. It is these *personal* qualities, rather than his or her physical organism, that constitute the real essence of humanity.

At this point Jesus introduces a truth that is fundamental if we are going to live by right standards and follow right practices. He assures us that the high value of human personality requires that we always and everywhere respect it. You dare not treat persons as though they were things, says the Master. You can't use them as mere instruments of your selfish purposes or of your evil passions.

When standards are disregarded, it is because values are being violated; and when values are being violated, we are degrading both ourselves and others. But now we must take a further step.

If Christian practice is tied to Christian standards, and the standards are tied to values, it must next be shown that *Christian values* are tied to the *Christian revelation of God*. We face here the colossal fact that Christianity claims to be the supreme revelation of the nature and the will of God.

According to the Bible, man and woman are creatures who started well and went wrong. God put them at the steering wheel and showed them the highway. Defiantly and foolishly they drove into the ditch. They have been floundering in the ditch ever since—except as they allow God's salvaging service to operate on their behalf.

Historically, the race of humanity who missed their way have been visited by God in many ways and in growing measures. Conscience was an early visit from God—the consciousness of right and wrong.

Furthermore—and this was a mighty development—God chose a particular people, the Hebrews, and for several centuries He beamed the truth to them that He was the sovereign Creator and the holy Judge of all people.

At long last, in what Scripture calls "the fulness of the time" (Gal. 4:4), He revealed himself by entering into a living union with human nature, in the person of Jesus of Nazareth, and so performing certain acts, openly and historically, upon which the salvation of humanity is said to depend. In Jesus He gave us the final unveiling of His holy yet loving character. In Jesus He demonstrated, by the Resurrection, His sovereign ability to overcome all foes, vindicate all His purposes, and provide us with a clue to His final triumph over evil throughout the length and breadth of His universe.

To summarize, this wisdom about life is not a simple thing; it is a system, a pattern. Starting with our visible life and working back to what is invisible, we have first our *practices,* our behaviors. Back of our practices, and governing them, are our *standards.* Back of our standards, and determining them, are our *values.* Back of our values, and giving them authority, is the *revelation* we see in Christ Jesus. Back of this revelation, and explaining it, is God!

As we began, so we close: "Whosoever heareth these sayings of mine, and doeth them, I will liken him unto a wise man, which built his house upon a rock" (Matt. 7:24). Draw your own conclusion. I have drawn mine: Jesus Christ makes sense!

6

THE "RATHERS" OF THE SPIRITUALLY-MINDED

WHAT IS YOUR UNDERSTANDING OF CHRISTIAN SPIRITUALITY? Do you judge it by the way people dress, or the slang that they avoid, or the shows that they shun, or the loudness with which they pray, or the ascetic isolation in which they live? Or how?

The apostle Paul does in fact speak of those who are "spiritually minded" (Rom. 8:6). Is there anything to indicate that he had in mind any of the tests we have indicated above—tests, it might be added, that from time to time have been applied by different Christian groups?

Let me try my hand at setting down some tests that I believe far more accurately reflect the view of both the apostle and his Lord.

The spiritually-minded would rather uphold Christ's reputation than their own. What happens to them is not so important as what happens to His good name that has been entrusted to them to cherish and guard.

The spiritually-minded would rather appear to lose an argument and keep their poise than to win an argument and lose their temper. Ill temper is the refuge of the insecure and the vain.

The spiritually-minded would rather look at everything from God's point of view than look at anything from their

39

own independent point of view. Their own opinions or sentiments give way before whatever clear light comes from Him through Jesus Christ.

The spiritually-minded would rather be holy than be happy. At the highest level the holy *are* the happy. But at secondary levels value judgments must be made in which mere pleasure or convenience have to yield to the pursuit of holiness.

The spiritually-minded would rather serve than be served. The hallmark of the service rendered is its style: not that of a superior but that of a servant. The superior doles out aid to an inferior; the servant follows his or her Servant-Lord in washing the feet of undeserving men and women.

The spiritually-minded would rather take God's free grace when the consequences are costly than take God's costly grace and cheapen it by making the consequences easy. "Cheap grace," as Bonhoeffer put it, "is the preaching of forgiveness without requiring repentance, baptism without church discipline, Communion without confession, absolution without contrition."

The spiritually-minded would rather be the intimates of God than to be the confidants of kings. Rarely is it possible to be both. The person who would be popular with the powerful of this world hazards his or her intimacy with the Prince of all worlds.

The spiritually-minded would rather be blessed with adversity than to be cursed with prosperity. They take seriously the Bible proverb "Better is a little with the fear of the LORD than great treasure and trouble with it" (Prov. 15:16, RSV).

The spiritually-minded would rather die for the right than to live for the wrong. They repudiate the rationalizing clichés by which others try to cover their shady practices: "After all, a person has to live, you know"; "Religion is all right, but business is business"; and the like.

The spiritually-minded would rather pass on real love to a visible person than to profess a spurious love for the invisible God. Phillips gives us this rendering of 1 John 4:20: "If a man says, 'I love God' and hates his brother, he is a liar. For if he does not love the brother before his eyes how can he love the one beyond his sight?"

A friend tells of a pastor on the West Coast who one day was rocketing along in his car on his way to his favorite spot for surfing. He shot past a longhaired hitchhiker, thinking to himself, "I hate these hippies." A moment or two later a flat tire halted him. By the time it was removed and the spare tire fitted on, the unwanted hitchhiker had caught up with the pastor. Could he ride? Well, yes, with the understanding that it would be for only a short distance.

Once they got rolling, the "hippie" startled the pastor by asking, "Could you be a minister?" Yes, he was. Then came the blow of real surprise for the man of God: "I gave my life to Jesus Christ a few days ago, but I need someone to tell me about living the Christian life."

Result? The inwardly shamed pastor forgot about his surfboard, pulled his car to the side of the highway, took a New Testament from the glove compartment, and held an absorbing conversation with the newly converted young man.

There was not spirituality in saying, "I hate hippies." There was profound spirituality in showing love to a particular hippie who needed Christian nurture even more than he needed a lift along the highway.

7

THINGS, THRALLS, AND THRILLS

SOMEONE HAS CALLED OURS A "THING-MINDED CIVILIZATION." Professor Sorokin, when he was teaching at Harvard, branded it as a "sensate culture." What he meant was that we are more engrossed in that part of living that stimulates the senses than we are in that part of it that concerns our intellectual and spiritual powers.

True, 20th-century humanity is not the first to be too dazzled by the fascination of material values. It was a British poet of the previous century who complained, "Things are in the saddle, and they ride mankind." And a greater than any poet long ago warned, "A man's life consisteth not in the abundance of the things which he possesseth" (Luke 12:15).

Yet things are here. The planet on which we live is a thing. We simply cannot escape things and relationships to things.

Our problem, therefore, is to determine what our relationship is to be. The Christian answer to the problem, broadly stated, is this: To the glory of God we are to control things without letting things control us. If they control us, they become thralls—fetters and thongs to bind and enslave us. If we, under God, control them, they become thrills—ours, not as masters but as servants. When this relationship is in effect, we are entitled to enter into the meaning of Paul's words: "Trust . . . in the living God, who giveth us richly all things to *enjoy*" (1 Tim. 6:17, emphasis added).

Let's say this about *things:*

1. God owns them. We don't. If our thinking misfires at this point, everything will come out wrongly. From the galaxies above our heads to the gravel beneath our feet, God is the Maker and Owner of all. The pride that denies this is as blind as it is brazen.

From this it follows that we are in trouble when we pay more attention to one's claim on that which is not his or her own than we do to God's claim on that which is His own.

2. God lends them. "For all things come of thee," said David in prayer, "and of thine own have we given thee" (1 Chron. 29:14).

Steward I, and not possessor—of the wealth intrusted me;
What, were God himself the Holder, would His disposition be?
This I ask myself each morning, every noon, and every night,
As I view His gentle goodness with an ever-new delight.

3. God will ask us what we did with them. Jesus made it clear that every servant and steward will be called to account. In that day of reckoning it will be *attitudes*, not *amounts*, that will be decisive.

> *It's not what you've done with a million,*
>   *If riches should e'er be your lot;*
> *But what are you doing at present,*
>   *With the dollar and quarter you've got?*

God owns things; God lends things; and God will ask what we did with things.

How, now, is all of this related to the idea of *thralls?* The answer may be found in something a popular newspaper philosopher once said. Sidney Harris wrote in the *Chicago Daily News:* "The oldest and saddest piece of wisdom in the world is that a man eventually becomes owned by his possessions. The ancient Greek philosophers and the biblical prophets warned against this subtle and dangerous form of slavery."

We are wise to remember that material possessions in relation to the soul are neutral. They can be a blessing or a blight, a curse or a contentment—all depending on how we use them. Treat things as ends, and you will become their master.

If you want to test yourself as to whether you are master or slave, try out the following questions: With more income and more material goods at my disposal, am I doing *proportionately* more or less for the kingdom of God? As matters stand now, if I were to die, how much of my estate would go to the *support* of the Christian Church and its far-flung activities?

And what shall we say of the thrills that send their tingle through the spirit of a man or woman who has discovered Christ's way to rule things and not to be ruled by them? The same Paul who told Timothy that God "giveth us richly all things to enjoy" (1 Tim. 6:17) instructed him, in the same passage, to tell the Christians who were "rich in this present world" that they were "to do good, to be rich in kindly actions, to be ready to give to others and to sympathize with those in distress" (vv. 17-18, PHILLIPS).

Once, while speaking at a conference in Emporia, Kansas, I was told of a day when the city of Emporia was dedicating a small, lovely park. It had been given to the citizens by the city's most famous townsman, William Allen White. The distinguished publisher, in making his simple presentation speech, said, "Today I am getting the last kick out of a handful of dollars. You know, there are three kicks in every dollar. First, there is the kick you get when you make it. I get that from my Scotch father. I do love to make a dollar. Secondly, there is the kick you get when you save it. I get that too from my Scotch father. Thirdly, there is the kick you get when you give it away. I get that from my mother, who was Irish. She gave with a free hand. It is this kick that is greatest of all."

Put God second and things first, and they will be your *enslavement*. Put God first and things second, and they will be your *enjoyment*.

PART II

Bountiful Resources

8

WHAT HE WAS MADE (CHRISTMAS SERMON)

A Sermon Classic

"THE WORD WAS MADE FLESH" (John 1:14).

"He hath made him to be sin for us" (2 Cor. 5:21).

"Whom God hath raised up" and "hath made . . . both Lord and Christ" (Acts 2:24, 36).

One of the most remarkable facts one confronts in his or her study of the New Testament is the varied yet unified witness that body of Scripture bears to our Lord Jesus Christ. In a half dozen scattered passages, set down by different writers, occurring in various connections, is an expression that has of late laid fast hold upon my thinking: He was "made"! John says He was "made flesh" (1:14). Paul says He was "made . . . to be sin" (2 Cor. 5:21), "made under the law" (Gal. 4:4), "made a curse" (3:13). The author of Hebrews observes that He was "made like unto his brethren" (2:17). Luke proclaims that He was made "alive" (24:23), and Peter adds that through His being made alive, He had been "made . . . both Lord and Christ" (Acts 2:36). What an oddly assorted and yet marvelously related series of affirmations! Studied reverently and believed devoutly, this many-voiced witness of the New Testament will give us an accurate and exalted view of the person of Him whose earthly advent we have come once more to celebrate.

Incidentally, we do well to remind ourselves of two things: first, that the person of the Christ is the heart of the Christian creed; and second, that there is no finer or more fitting time than Christmas for taking stock of our views of Him.

There are three revelations concerning Him and what He was made that shall claim our major attention for this hour. Some related passages will serve to enlighten and enforce the truth of these larger unfoldings.

John declares that He was made flesh—and there you have the great *Incarnation*.

Paul states that He was made sin—and there you have the great *Salvation*.

Peter announces that He was made alive—and there you have the great *Resurrection*.

1. HE WAS MADE FLESH

"The Word was made flesh, and dwelt among us" (John 1:14).

The tremendous meaning of these words can be glimpsed only against the background of the 13 preceding verses—verses which, if hurriedly read, are sure to escape us. Consider two or three of the peaks in that background. "The Word *was* God" (v. 1, emphasis added). Thus are we shown the Christ of essential deity. Mind you, He did not have to be "made" God. He was that. Take another: "The Word was *with* God" (v. 1, emphasis added). By this fine turn of language we are shown the Christ of the Trinity, co-equal with God and yet differentiated from Him in that mysterious distinguishment that belongs to Father, Son, and Holy Ghost in the unity of the triune Godhead. Then consider this: *"In the beginning* was the Word" (v. 1, emphasis added). Here we have the Christ of eternity. Christ of deity! Christ of the Trinity! Christ of eternity! This Being was never made at all. His divinity did not evolve. Nobody elected Him to His place in the Godhead. He had neither birthday nor birthplace. "In the beginning." Write that across His deity. Write it across His Sonship. Write it across the unwritten page of the unrecorded past, back there before the centuries moved out in chronicled order or the millennia began their measured march.

And now emerges the marvel. He who was God, uncreated, underived, unbegun, was made flesh. Flesh! That is the Word. Flesh like yours and mine—eyes, ears, hands, feet! Such is the teaching of Scripture. Such is the faith of the Church. The eternal has invaded the temporal. The Creator has assumed creaturehood. The Christ of eternity has become the Jesus of history. The everlasting Son of God has united His own divine nature with a true human nature in the unity of a single personality.

Virgin Birth. If the Virgin Birth is the fact of the Incarnation, what light have the Scriptures to throw upon that fact, its method, and its meaning? Two apostolic utterances are of special significance in this connection. Paul is on record as saying that Christ was "made of a woman" (Gal. 4:4), while the author of the Hebrews declares that he was "made like unto his brethren" (2:17). Both passages, it will be seen, have to do with His being made flesh.

The Galatians word points to the medium of our Lord's entry into the order of human life and the stream of human history. He came by the ministry of human brotherhood. And that ministry fell to a virgin. It was said of her that she was "blessed . . . among women" (Luke 1:42). It was said concerning her maiden motherhood, "That holy thing which [was] born of [her was] the Son of God" (v. 35). Respecting her, it had been said prophetically, "Behold, a virgin shall conceive, and bear a son, and shall call his name Immanuel" (Isa. 7:14). "And the angel said unto her, Fear not, Mary: for thou hast found favour with God. And, behold, thou shalt conceive in thy womb, and bring forth a son, and shalt call his name JESUS. . . . Then said Mary unto the angel, How shall this be, seeing I know not a man? And the angel answered and said unto her, The Holy Ghost shall come upon thee, and the power of the Highest shall overshadow thee: therefore also that holy thing which shall be born of thee shall be called the Son of God" (Luke 1:30-31, 34-35).

Admit a real Incarnation, accept the fact that Jesus is "very God of very God," and the appearance of the supernatural in connection with His earth advent will harmonize perfectly with the character of the occurrence. The revelation of the miraculous will stumble no one who believes that the infinite God has actually stooped to such voluntary limiting of himself as is necessary to life in human form.

A King but a Comrade. "Made of a woman." If this describes the origin of His life in the flesh, the statement that He was "made like unto his brethren" suggests the development of that life. God would find a basis for helping and redeeming humanity by entering, within limits, into a community of experience. He does not stoop to our sins; He does stoop to the level of the life in which our sins make their appearance, and there He reveals His perfect manhood. In Christ He would seek comradeship with us— "that he might be a merciful and faithful high priest" (Heb. 2:17). He comes where we are in our hungers and thirsts and pains, our temptations and struggles and sorrows, our labors and losses and limitations. If Albert of Belgium, king though he was, could not stay away from the front when his soldiers were daring death to save the nation, if something noble within him made him share the grim life of his embattled, shell-torn armies, some of us dare to believe that the God whom we worship could not remain out of the human struggle. Love impelled Him to make contact with us and to thrust himself into the battle, which He did, and, blessed be His name, has become forevermore the deciding factor in the conflict.

So we have Him—"made flesh," "made of a woman," "made like unto his brethren." Not God *and* man, nor God *in* man, but the one and only *God-man*; so human that He got thirsty, so divine that He could say, "If any man thirst, let him come unto me, and drink. He that believeth on me, as the scripture hath said, out of his belly shall flow rivers of living water" (John 7:37-38); so human that He got hungry, so divine that He took five loaves and two fishes and spread a banquet for 5,000 men and their famished families; so human that He grew weary and dropped down onto a well curb, so divine He could say, "Come unto me, all ye that labour and are heavy laden, and I will give you rest" (Matt. 11:28); so human He must needs have sleep, so divine He rose from that sleep to turn back with a word the fury of a tempest and to spread a perfect peace on the face of a raging sea; so human He found it needful to have seasons of prayer, so divine that never once was He under necessity to make confession of sin; so human He yearned for the sympathy of men and women and felt the pangs of loneliness, so divine He declared 12 legions of angels waited to take wing to His side; so human He grew in wisdom and stature, so divine that in Him dwelt "all the fulness of the Godhead bodily" (Col. 2:9).

2. HE WAS MADE SIN

"For he hath made him to be sin for us, who knew no sin; that we might be made the righteousness of God in him" (2 Cor. 5:21).

With us goodness is relative; with Jesus goodness is absolute. He was not only good but sinlessly good. The fact of His sinlessness, established beyond question if we accept the record, is as morally unique as His birth is physically solitary. No voice ever spoke more unsparingly against sin, particularly the sins of religious leaders, than did that of John the Baptist, yet to Jesus he said, "I have need to be baptized of thee, and comest thou to me?" (Matt. 3:14). It was the honest verdict of Pilate: "I find no fault in him" (John 19:4). Judas, unwilling to die with accursed pelf in his palm and an accursed lie on his lips, cried, "I have betrayed the innocent blood" (Matt. 27:4). In the presence of His foes the Galilean could throw down the challenge "Which of you convinceth me of sin?" (John 8:46).

The Bearer of Sin. And He who was as reproachless and stainless as this was "made . . . sin for us" (2 Cor. 5:21). We the sinful! He the sinless! We the guilty! He the guiltless! If you can in some measure grasp this, you are ready for the logical sequence that lies in Paul's statement that He was "made a curse" (Gal. 3:13). If He is "made . . . sin," He must be "made a curse," for that is what sin is. Made sin—for us! Made a curse—for you, for me! Never a curse *to* anybody, He becomes a curse *for* everybody.

Watch Him now. He is gathering into His own heart the mystery of evil, the pain of it, the woe of it, the awfulness of it, yes—let us not blink at the fact—the damnableness of it, and is carrying it to a Cross. The physical suffering is intense, but the mental and moral pain is infinitely worse. He gave His body, but He gave more. His "soul [was made] an offering for sin" (Isa. 53:10). His soul! For the soul is the seat of sin, and the body the instrument of the soul.

Hear Him now: "My God, my God, why hast thou forsaken me?" (Matt. 27:46). Just what took place in that moment you and I shall never know. It is quite beyond us. In the vivid language of Frederick Shannon, "We believe that the Lord of Glory went mysteriously out into the waste places of sin, tasting the bitter drops of the second death and the first." The final issue of final sin is Godforsakenness. He was made sin. He therefore tasted that unutterable agony of the Father's withdrawal—and tasted it unto death!

Yet, paradoxical as it may seem, God was never nearer than in those bleeding moments before the death of the Cross. He was in Christ. It was He who gave His love and life there. Now hear Him: "It is finished" (John 19:30). "It is finished!" There is death, but it is the death that gives birth to life. There is defeat, but it is the defeat that conquers. There is the mystery of atonement. A Savior has come, mighty to save and strong to deliver. Being made sin, He becomes sin's Destroyer. Being made a curse *for* us, He lifts the curse *from* us.

It is all a part of the ageless, fadeless Christmas story, for the manger and the Cross are inseparable. He was made flesh in order that He might be made sin. The world's hope, its one lone, trembling hope, lay cradled in that Bethlehem grotto. It rose in steady ascent until it reached the summit of the skull-shaped hill and broke in splendor from Joseph's garden tomb.

> *That night when in the Judean skies*
> *The mystic star dispensed its light,*
> *A blind man moved in his sleep—*
> *And dreamed that he had sight.*
>
> *That night when shepherds heard the song*
> *Of hosts angelic choiring near,*
> *A deaf man stirred in slumber's spell—*
> *And dreamed that he could hear!*
>
> *That night when in the cattle stall*
> *Slept Child and mother cheek by jowl,*
> *A cripple turned his twisted limbs—*
> *And dreamed that he was whole.*
>
> *That night when o'er the newborn Babe*
> *The tender Mary rose to lean,*
> *A loathsome leper smiled in sleep—*
> *And dreamed that he was clean.*

That night when to the mother's breast
The little King was held secure,
A harlot slept a happy sleep—
And dreamed that she was pure!

That night when in the manger lay
The Sanctified Who came to save,
A man moved in the sleep of death—
And dreamed there was no grave.

Nor did they dream in vain. Christ is more than any soul has ever dreamed. He is the heart's dream come true. He is the world's Hope fulfilled.

3. HE WAS MADE ALIVE

"He shewed himself alive after his passion" (Acts 1:3). And as the Risen One, declared Peter, He is "made . . . both Lord and Christ" (2:36).

A Dead King? There He hangs, a kingly inscription over His head, but dead. "Whatever He was, whoever He was, He is dead now"—one can hear them say it. Those scribes and elders whose lifeless creeds and showy forms He had condemned for their emptiness were glad enough. He was dead! The proud Pharisees who had smarted under His terrific indictments and who had cunningly plotted to dispatch Him were pleased enough. He was dead! The callous soldiery, hardened servants of a heartless government, having driven the nails and planted the Cross and held the rabble at bay, were eager to gamble for His cloak. He was dead!

The disciples and relatives faced the same grim fact, but with what different eyes they looked upon it! That form beloved that they had seen move through street and lane, over sea and field and hill—that form had stiffened. Those hands so tireless in labor, so often lifted in benediction, so many times extended in mercy—those hands were motionless. Those eyes that had oftentimes met their earnest gaze

56

with sympathy, tenderness, and understanding—those eyes were now glazed. And their grief was beyond measuring. It was a bereavement in which hope offered them no sweet ministry of succour, for hope with them died when their Lord did. "For as yet they knew not the scripture, that he must rise again from the dead" (John 20:9).

Then something happened, something so amazingly great, something so transcendently marvelous that, whether He actually arose or not, Christianity has a miracle lodged at her roots. If the miracle of His resurrection be denied, there is a greater wonder to be explained. It is the wonder of a handful of ordinary Galileans so sure that they had seen and communed with the risen Jesus that they went forth to preach Him with a passion no waters could quench and to dare death in a hundred forms if only they might give testimony to their faith in Him as the Son of God and the Redeemer of the world.

They were sure—and so are we. They worshiped a living Savior—and likewise we. For Joseph's tomb is empty, the air is filled with music, and at the right hand of the Majesty sits a risen and enthroned Lord Christ. How do we know? Well, by the external, historic evidences, for one thing. They are convincing enough to all but the hopelessly prejudiced. But better still, we know Him alive by the internal witness of His presence in our hearts. He must be alive, because He makes us live. He must be a living Person, for He exerts a living power in the souls of individuals.

The Artist's Touch. There is in the history of art a rather unique illustration of this truth. For years critics have argued whether the painting titled *The Virgin of the Rocks*, hanging in the National Gallery in London, is a genuine work of Leonardo da Vinci. There is one almost identically like it in the Louvre in Paris, and it is an unquestioned da Vinci. The English gallery paid $45,000 for its painting. Were they swindled, or is it a true product of the celebrated Italian master? It is now claimed that the dispute is settled. The story is an interesting one. Charles Holmes, an authority on art, had discovered that much of the exquisite effect of da Vinci's work with oil had been produced by softening the still-wet paint with finger and thumb tips. With this knowledge he set about his task in a perfectly scientific fashion. He selected a half dozen da Vincis about which there was not doubt. Officers from Scotland Yard then examined the fingerprints, after which they journeyed to Paris, where they tested the unchallenged *Virgin of the Rocks.* They then returned to London, took the fingerprints of the debated picture, made their careful comparisons, and pronounced it genuine.

What made their decision possible? It was the touch of the artist still upon the canvas after the passing of four centuries. Do you ask how we know Christ rose and lives? By His touch upon our souls, we answer, by His touch upon our souls! A touch that quickens! A touch that heals! A touch that transfigures! A touch that makes old things die and new things leap into life! For

> *Warm, sweet, tender, even yet*
> *A present Help is He;*
> *And faith has still its Olivet*
> *And love its Galilee.*

> *The healing of His seamless dress*
> *Is by our beds of pain;*
> *We touch Him in life's throng and press,*
> *And we are whole again.*
>
> —John Greenleaf Whittier

Yes, He touches us, and we touch Him; so do we know that He was "made alive" (1 Cor. 15:22). And so you may know it. What could you do that would more appropriately celebrate the Savior's birth than to open your heart to Him this very day—yes, this very moment? Confess to Him your unworthiness and your sinfulness. Let Him speak to your trusting heart the word of His forgiveness and peace. If you will do this, Bethlehem will not seem so far away. Instead of being a dim and distant point in history, it will glow in your heart as the symbol of new life through Christ Jesus the Lord.

9

Don't Panic—
Believe!

I HAVE JUST COME FROM THE CEMETERY. He was 85—and ready to go. We had known each other for nearly half a century. Before he knew me, he had known my father. He had requested that I take the sermon at his funeral.

What I offered to the relatives and friends was John 14:1-2. It has a quiet, golden eloquence that nearly 20 centuries have never stilled: "Let not your heart be troubled: ye believe in God, believe also in me. In my Father's house are many mansions: if it were not so, I would have told you. I go to prepare a place for you."

Shall I tell you what I said, standing there beside that sealed coffin? Without apology, I made the claim that our Lord opened up the fourfold secret of an untroubled heart in a troubled world. Not an *unfeeling* heart, mind you; but an *unoverwhelmed* heart, if we may so express it.

Believe in God the Father, who created you. "Ye believe in God," said Jesus to these men of the Hebrew faith. They did. From their youth they had affirmed, "The LORD our God is one LORD" (Deut. 6:4); "In the beginning God created the heaven and the earth" (Gen. 1:1); "The LORD [is] our maker" (Ps. 95:6).

This is the foundation of everything. H. G. Wells was capable of saying stupid things, but he was on target when he wrote, "Unless a man believes in God, he starts from no beginning and he works to no end."

Believe in God the Son, who has redeemed you. When Jesus said, "Believe also in me," He was saying something that went beyond the *existence* of God to the *revelation* of God.

A boy stood alone one day in the drawing room of an elegant home, gazing up at the large portrait of his father, who had recently died. Unaware that he was being overheard by his mother, he finally said, "Daddy, I wish you would step down out of the frame and speak to me!" The ache of those words was not lost on the mother.

That boy was a symbol. He represented the whole human family before Christ came. The brilliant Plato had already said, "We look for a God, or a God-inspired man, who will show us ourselves and take away the darkness from our eyes." Here was the plea that God would step down from His vast cosmic "frame" and speak to people.

This He did in Jesus Christ. Such, at any rate, is the Christian claim. "He that hath seen me hath seen the Father" (John 14:9). "The Son of man is come to seek and to save that which was lost" (Luke 19:10). A spoiled creation has been given a strong Redeemer.

This man whose memory we were honoring had been a lover of old hymns. He knew them by heart. One of them, which I had once heard him singing softly while he was working in his home, was an Isaac Watts composition:

> *Not all the blood of beasts,*
> *   On Jewish altars slain,*
> *Could give the guilty conscience peace,*
> *   Or wash away its stain.*
> *But Christ, the heavenly Lamb,*
> *   Takes all our sins away;*
> *A sacrifice of nobler name,*
> *   And richer blood than they.*

It was a kindly and perceptive old monk who once said to the conscience-tortured Martin Luther, "We must believe not only in the forgiveness of David's sins and Peter's sins but also that our own sins are forgiven."

Exactly that is what we do believe when we believe on Christ our Savior.

Believe in God the Holy Spirit, who lives in you. As an essential part of our Lord's message in John 14, He said, "I will pray the Father, and he shall give you another Comforter, that he may abide with you for ever. . . . He dwelleth with you, and shall be in you" (vv. 16-17).

If the Jesus of history is God *for* us, the Holy Spirit is God *in* us. He is God in us for the purpose of making real what Christ planned, and provided, and prayed for, on behalf of His people. "Keep them from the evil" (John 17:15)—the Holy Spirit is the Answer to the prayer. "Sanctify them" (v. 17)—the Holy Spirit is the Answer to that prayer. "That they all may be one" (v. 21)—the Holy Spirit is the Answer to that prayer. "That the world [through their united witness and work] may believe that thou hast sent me" (ibid.)—the Holy Spirit is the Answer to that prayer.

So it was believed by the servant of Christ whom we were honoring. So it must be believed by us the living, who are left behind.

Believe that there is a heavenly destiny that awaits you. Jesus called heaven "my Father's house." That is simple enough to be understandable.

He said of heaven that it has "many dwelling-places" (John 14:2, NEB). That is spacious enough to be unmeasurable.

He said, "If it were not so, I would have told you" (ibid.). This is sure enough to be unmistakable.

Here is no blueprint of details, but a bracing prospect of realities assured. Here is no "pie in the sky when you die," but eternal fulfillment of the life begun in Christ amid the tasks and tests of this world.

So don't panic! Believe!

That's what I said. And that, I am bound to affirm, is what needs to be said.

10

WHEN WAITING IS WINNING

THE VITALITY THAT COMES TO US through conversation and communion with God has its own varied patterns and rhythms. How else can we understand Isaiah when he describes for us the consequences of that praying that renews strength? "They shall mount up with wings as eagles; they shall run, and not be weary; and they shall walk, and not faint" (40:31).

The prophet's order of thought is remarkable—not *walk, run, fly,* but *fly, run, walk.*

There is strength for *soaring high.* Not always, but with great frequency, the initial effect of any powerful contact with God is of the order and nature of a rapture, a high elevation of our emotions.

In Bunyan's account of Christian in *The Pilgrim's Progress* is that famous passage in which Christian loses his burden at the Cross: "Then was Christian glad and lightsome, and said, with a merry heart, 'He hath given me rest by his sorrow, and life by his death.'" Christian leaps for joy and goes on singing: "Blest cross! blest sepulchre! blest rather be / The man that there was put to shame for me!"

Or one thinks of A. B. Simpson, flaming missionary spirit, founder of the Christian and Missionary Alliance, who, after being a fettered, frustrated Christian for years, had a crucial confrontation with his Lord. He later wrote, "Throwing myself at the feet of the glorious Master, I claimed the mighty promise—'I will dwell in you and walk in you.' Across the threshold of my spirit there passed a Being as real as the Christ who came to John on Patmos, and from that moment, a new secret has been the charm and glory and strength of my life and testimony."

Here is the *"mounting up"* phase, the "wings as eagles" aspect, of the life of God in the soul of man. It is the real "high" whose unmanning counterfeit is the artificiality and cruelty of the drug experience in today's society.

Waiting on God has another dimension: it gives strength for *surging ahead.* Isaiah knows that they who let God possess them will not always fly. What then? "They shall run, and not be weary."

The Bible makes running a figure of speech for the eagerness of devotion. This, we learn, applies to enthusiasm for evil as well as good. We read of those who "run to evil" (59:7), who are "swift to shed blood" (Rom. 3:15), who "run after strong drink" (Isa. 5:11, RSV).

More frequently the figure has a happy connotation. "I will run in the way of thy commandments" (Ps. 119:32, RSV), says the psalmist. "I do not run aimlessly" (1 Cor. 9:26, RSV), declares Paul. "So run, that ye may obtain . . . the prize" (v. 24), he exhorts the Corinthians. Even God's eagerness to reclaim His alienated children finds a mirror in the action of the father who "ran and embraced" the repentant son returning from red lights and pigsties (Luke 15:20, RSV).

Devotion to Christ is normally inseparable from devotion to people, for Christ is a people lover and a people carer. This devotion bends you forward, which is the posture of the swift runner.

This indeed is mission, whether ordained or spontaneous. It is the untiring eagerness to let the whole world know that, in the light of what God has done for us in Christ, life's ultimate word is not guilt but forgiveness, not hate but love, not cruelty but kindness, not discord but harmony, not despair but hope.

Isaiah is not finished until he has said something else about the value of waiting on God: it gives strength for *slogging on*. The term "slog on" is a phrase that, I believe, we owe to the British soldiers in World War I. When the going was incredibly tough in the mud of Flanders, there was nothing to do, they said, but to slog on. The phrase is terse and telling. In the intervals between the raptures and when running for the time being is impossible, still we can "walk, and not faint" (40:31).

If life in Christ is occasionally *crisis* and mostly *process*, then we'd better learn to be good pedestrians. "Walk in love" (Eph. 5:2), said Paul to the Ephesians. "Walk as children of light" (v. 8), he went on to tell them. "Walk circumspectly" (v. 15). "Walk worthy of the vocation ['calling,' RSV]" (4:1) that you have from Christ. Pedestrian tasks. Pedestrian responsibilities. Pedestrian challenges. But inescapably necessary.

It is chiefly at the walking pace that we learn what community is—how to relate to each other, how to take time for each other.

It is the slogging side of discipleship that exhibits the glory of the commonplace God with us in the daily round where hands are plunged in dishwater, feet are caked with mud, eyes are tired from fine print, and hearts are aching for "the touch of a vanished hand, / And the sound of a voice that is still!" (Tennyson).

There is little point in trying to improve on Isaiah's formula: put all the rhythms of your experience—the *soarings*, the *surgings*, the *sloggings*—under God's control. Wait upon Him. Be open to Him. Make time for Him.

In the waiting is hidden the secret of winning.

11

EMPOWERED WITNESSES

FOR EVERY ORDAINED MINISTER the Church needs a *hundred*, and for every theological professor a *thousand*, lay witnesses who will communicate the Good News and back it with their committed lives.

When the first Christians got so filled with the Holy Spirit that some of the citizens thought them stark mad, they made converts on the right hand and on the left, achieving results that a "cultural Christianity," silent and supine, can never so much as approach.

Jesus was pointed about it: "Ye shall receive power, after that the Holy Ghost is come upon you: and ye shall be witnesses unto me" (Acts 1:8).

Luke was equally pointed in recording the fulfillment of the promise: "And they were all filled with the Holy Ghost, and began to speak" (Acts 2:4).

And with *that* they were off! Off to disciple winning and life changing and church planting! Before long it was said of them: "These that have turned the world upside down are come hither also" (17:6).

The complacent, sterile, nonproductive church member of today is a long sea mile from the witnessing fellowship that was looked upon as such a revolutionary thing almost 20 centuries ago.

What to do?

Are we to conclude that power for a redemptively convincing and contagious discipleship has been withdrawn from the Christian community? Who can seriously believe it—or rest content with it? Is it not better to side with a friend who out of long years of dealing with stumbling, faltering souls says, "I am perfectly sure that spiritual help and power are as available to us as water or electricity"?

What, then, are some of the factors that *condition* and *accompany* God's power release, through the Holy Spirit, in the witnessing Christian or the witnessing group?

Heading the list, let's put *eagerness*. "Blessed are they which do hunger and thirst" (Matt. 5:6). Vague wishfulness is not enough. Ardent desire is prerequisite. People who are keener to learn how to raise rabbits, or win prizes with tulips, or to play a good hand at canasta than they are to be channels of converting power to beaten men and women about them should not be surprised if they remain on the list of the "noneffective" in the Church's ranks. They should not wonder if the whole vocabulary and spiritual apparatus of Pentecost remain foreign to them. When desire ravishes us, God's power will reach us.

Another factor in power release is *openness*—vertically toward God, horizontally toward people. The W. J. Conybeare translation of 2 Cor. 6:12-13 is an immense improvement on the King James Version: "You find no narrowness in my love," says Paul, "but the narrowness is in your own. I pray you therefore in return for my affection (I speak as to my children), let your hearts be opened in like manner."*

It isn't that we are *fated* to be spiritually small and ineffectual; rather, alas, it is that we are *contented* to be. Many

---

*W. J. Conybeare, *The Epistles of Paul: A Translation and Notes* (Grand Rapids: Baker Book House, 1958).

of us would begin writing a new chapter in our lives if we would break down in two simple ways: (1) in *praying* our hearts out to God; and (2) in *talking* our hearts out to some vital, soul-winning Christian we know and respect.

Then, surely, there is a close relation between released power and *cleanliness* in the life of the Christian. "Be ye clean, that bear the vessels of the LORD" (Isa. 52:11). There is a crass hedonism whose chief concern may be summed up in the words "Eat, drink, and be merry" (Luke 12:19). But there is a more subtle hedonism that currently may be gathered up in the magic phrase "peace of mind." Neither one matches the New Testament, where invariably the passion for holiness gets a higher rating than the quest for happiness. I can count on God to let power loose in my life when I am ready to let something loose—the hurtful habit, the crippling compromise, the unsurrendered ambition, the stubborn resentment, to which I have been clinging.

Still another factor that makes for spiritual power release in the life of the witnessing Christian is what may be called *directedness*. By this we mean the willingness not to use the Spirit's power as we wish or for our ends, but rather to let the Spirit use us for God's purposes and glory. A whimsical saint was commenting on the scripture in Isa. 41 in which Israel, having been called a "worm" (v. 14), is told that she will "thresh the mountains" (v. 15). Said he, "Of course God can take a worm and thresh a mountain, provided the worm will wiggle when He says wiggle!" Behind the humor is sober reality.

A scientist, whose nominal Christianity had blazed into something splendidly experiential and vital, was just beginning the witnessing life. One night, at two in the morning, an alcoholic was brought to his door. The friend who brought him said, "I know you can help him." There was momentary reluctance in his heart. "Lord," he murmured half aloud, "is this what I have to do?" to which his wife made the querying comment, "What would Jesus do?"

It was enough. From two o'clock till six the man worked on the derelict whom drink had ravaged. Then victory! A beaten, enchained man born again by the power of the Spirit of God! But the power flowed through a channel that was flexible enough to be directed.

Empowered witnesses! Inspect them wherever you find them. You are pretty certain to find that they are eager souls, transparently open, sensitive to sin and in no mood to compromise with it, holding their witness not as a sort of monopoly for them to control but as a trust for the Holy Spirit to manage—and use.

12

THE ART
OF THE HEART

WHEN PRESIDENT ULYSSES S. GRANT LAY DYING, old friend
Gen. O. O. Howard came to see him. Howard told his old
chief, under whom he had fought through the Civil War,
how much the people of the United States appreciated his
work. Grant, restless and wistful, seemed unimpressed.
What had impressed him, obviously, was the example of
faith and prayer that Howard had long set before his fellow officers and soldiers. "Tell me," cut in the dying com-
mander in chief, "tell me something more about prayer."

It is a piercingly appropriate request, spurred alike by
humility and by hope. Always there is something more to
learn about this amazing function and force by means of
which, as Alfred, Lord Tennyson put it, "more things are
wrought . . . than this world dreams of."

Prayer is *responsive*. At one level it may be ignorance
and fear responding to mystery, littleness responding to
vastness, guilt of violated taboo responding to a terror
world of spirits manipulated by medicine men and witch
doctors. At a different level it may be the disciple of Jesus,
awed by His own practice of prayer into a reverential
aching of wonder and longing, saying wistfully, "Lord,
teach us to pray" (Luke 11:1).

In prayer, God is always there ahead of us. He is the

prior fact. He tirelessly cultivates the prayers of His biblically enlightened people. "Call to me and I will answer you" (Jer. 33:3, RSV).

Prayer is *purgative*. Christian prayer is an invited intimacy with the Father God, who is loving and holy. In His presence the pride that is discovered is the pride that dies. The resentment that is cancerous is the resentment that is cured. The pettiness that is probed is the pettiness that is purged. Contrite and believing prayer is the soul's immersion in the sacrificial "mind of Christ" (1 Cor. 2:16), who on the Cross made His pure soul an offering for our sin. "The blood of Jesus Christ his Son cleanseth us from all sin" (1 John 1:7).

Prayer is *expansive*. It is Isaiah in the Temple, convicted and concerned with his own discovered need, but not resting there—going on, instead, to see with sharpened vision the needs of others near and far and to say to God, "Send me" (6:8). It is the disciples, under the tutoring of Jesus, being told, "Lift up your eyes, and see how the fields are already white for harvest" (John 4:35, RSV); "Pray ye therefore the Lord of the harvest, that he will send forth labourers into his harvest" (Matt. 9:38).

Prayer widens the walls of the heart. It gives an interior spaciousness. "Prayer," wrote S. D. Gordon when the 20th century was young, "opens a whole planet to man's activities. I can, in reality, be touching hearts for God in faraway India or China through prayer as though I were there. . . . A man may go aside today and shut his door . . . and, in reality, spend a half hour of his life in India for God as though he were there in person."

Do you doubt that? If you do, there is no mathematical calculus by which you can be convinced. Those who know the art of the heart, which is loving intercession, will not doubt it. To them prayer is not saying, "Tell You what I'll do, God. Let's make a deal!" Prayer, on the contrary, is being caught up into the *livingness* of the "God and Father of our Lord Jesus Christ" and participating in His purpose of reconciliation for proud, ego-centered humans of every ilk.

If S. D. Gordon spoke his world-encircling mind to an earlier generation, George Arthur Buttrick confronted our own time when he wrote, "So honest prayer is linked with life. We pray, and then speak the unpopular word. . . . We pray, and then we both vote and labor against politicians who play both ends against the middle, and thus sidestep the demand of a revolutionary time. . . . Yet prayer is not committed to any ism, for all isms are transient and open to human sin. . . . Our activisms are both blind and compulsive without prayer."

Prayer, then, is *mission.* It is not an adjunct to mission. It belongs. It is an integral part of it. It brings the world within our ken. It lays the world upon our heart. It broadens our sympathies and empathies into a vital participation in the whole community of Christ's witnessing servants.

13

SALVATION'S WAY

FOUR GUIDING TERMS MOVE US ALONG THE WAY OF GRACE that is luminously marked out in the words of 1 John 1:9: "If we confess our sins, he is faithful and just to forgive us our sins, and to cleanse us from all unrighteousness." They are (1) *conviction*, (2) *confession*, (3) *cancellation*, and (4) *cleansing*.

Conviction. "If we confess our sins," says John. But who is going to confess sins of whose sinfulness and wrong he or she has no deep and arousing sense? Back of, and beneath, all true repentance is an awakened conscience, an illumination by the Word of God and the Spirit of God upon the reality of sin as that which offends holiness and love.

Men and women will not be saved until they profoundly feel their need of salvation. Nor will they feel their need of salvation until they are smitten through with a realization of the hurt and the hell created by their pride and rebellion—a realization that is all too rare in these morally flabby days.

We have gone to the devil's dictionary for new and misleading terms with which to dress up old and ugly sins. Lying is "smartness." Adultery and immorality are merely "sex adventures." Smut and obscenity are given the false dignity of "frankness." Theft and robbery pass as "unadjusted acquisitiveness."

Yet cover and camouflage it as we will, sin remains the

74

same dark, deadly, destructive thing that it is. This, accordingly, is where we begin. Conviction of sin is the first step in salvation.

Confession. "If we confess our sins." Mind you, *confess.* It is one thing to *admit* you are a sinner; it is decidedly another thing to *confess* it. One is often done with a smile; the other, more often than not, with a sob. Some will neither admit nor confess. They cover. They deny. But when the condemning conviction of the Spirit of God rests upon them, they are in wretchedness of mind and heart.

Is there not after all a very general misunderstanding of the true nature and significance of confession of sin? I am bound to believe there is—else we should not have so many soul-blighting concealments and mind-maddening repressions.

Confession is no part of the punishment of sin; it is the way of release from its burden. If you are looking for analogies, do not think of it as an assassin's dagger—think of it as a surgeon's knife. It is an instrument of incision for draining away virulent poison. It may hurt a bit, but the alternative is everlasting moral invalidism and spiritual death. It is the patient's one sure way of relief and recuperation.

David wrote, "When I kept silence, my bones waxed old through my roaring all the day long. For day and night thy hand was heavy upon me: my moisture is turned into the drought of summer" (Ps. 32:3-4). What strange and haunting language this is! Hidden sin! Sealed lips! The roaring tempest of inward conflict! The unrelaxing pressure of a mighty hand reaching down from above! And the result? Bones waxing old! Premature aging! Moisture turned into the drought of summer! The juices of genuine, joyous living turned off!

And David became desperate. The next verse records the outcome: "I acknowledged my sin unto thee, and mine iniquity have I not hid. I said, I will confess my transgressions unto the LORD; and thou forgavest the iniquity of my sin" (v. 5). Old as this ancient record is, its very words breathe with a sense of that immense relief that came to the heart of the psalmist.

Cancellation. Confession thus made needs only to have added the faith that receives the gracious work of promise to which we now come: "He is faithful and just to forgive us our sins." If there is no music in that sentence, the universe holds no melody in all its cheerless spaces!

God has declared himself. He is "faithful" to forgive. That is, He is true, dependably and absolutely true, to His character of love and to His promises of mercy. "Let the wicked forsake his way, and the unrighteous man his thoughts: and let him return unto the LORD, and he will have mercy upon him; and to our God, for he will abundantly pardon" (Isa. 55:7). More certain than the rising and setting of suns is this glorious pledge of pardon. God is faithful!

Moreover, He is "just" to forgive. Forgiveness as a matter of justice! Think of what a strange putting of it this is. To understand it, we must go to the Cross. God's love is a holy love and must express itself in keeping with the character of sin. To offer an easy forgiveness for sin is to minimize it if not to sanction it. Since God could do neither, His measureless, matchless love for the sinner decided Him upon another course, with the result that the Cross, which He had perpetually worn in His heart since man's first disobedience, was lifted visibly and symbolically at Calvary, and that once and for all.

Sacrifice unto death is there, for sin is so terrible a thing that God must pay dearly for grappling with it. Atonement is there, full and complete. Righteousness is there, its claim fully met. Love is there, streaming in crimson, compassionate courses. And in view of it all, the assurance of our acquittal has been written down in this incontestable document that we call the holy Word of God.

Cleansing. "And to cleanse us from all unrighteousness." Full redemption is the Calvary message and the New Testament revelation. The God who justifies will also sanctify. "The blood of Jesus Christ his Son cleanseth us from all sin" (1 John 1:7).

"Blessed are they which do hunger and thirst after righteousness" (Matt. 5:6) is the benediction we should be able to pronounce upon every man, woman, or child who has been genuinely converted. And to all such is held out the promise "They shall be filled" (ibid.). Having been cleansed from all unrighteousness, they will be filled with the pure love of God.

To put the distinction between forgiveness and cleansing as clearly as possible, let me suggest the following contrasts: Forgiveness is a judicial act; cleansing is a priestly ministry. Forgiveness takes place in the heart of God; cleansing takes place in the heart of the believer. Forgiveness deals with the wrong I have done; cleansing deals with the wrong I *am.* What I have done is volitional; what I *am* is dispositional. Forgiveness gives me standing before God; cleansing gives me fellowship with God. Forgiveness makes me an heir; cleansing gives me an inheritance among them who are sanctified. Forgiveness provides peace with God; cleansing imparts the peace of God.

One man's prayer might well be the prayer of all: "Lord, I want to be as clean as the blood of Christ can make a redeemed sinner."

14

DARE TO
BE EXPECTANT!

FOUR HUNDRED YEARS AGO the first Englishman to sail around the world completed his achievement and fulfilled his dream. His name was Francis Drake.

One of Drake's biographers speaks of him as one who had always looked out on life as though he expected doors to open before him, "through which he would pass to magic realms and great experiences."

He expected doors to open, and they did!

Come to think about it, the Bible has a good deal to say about this attitude of positive expectancy. Take, for example, the healing of the lame beggar about which we are told in Acts 3. In verses 2 and 5 we read, "And a certain man lame from his mother's womb . . . gave heed unto them [Peter and John], *expecting* to receive something of them" (emphasis added).

True, his expectancy level was probably low—nothing more than a pittance from the coins he hoped these men were carrying. The point is that it was *positive.*

The further point is that it was a response to what one of them had said: "Look on us" (v. 4). Then from Peter came words that displayed his own much higher level of expectancy: "Silver and gold have I none; but such as I have give I thee: In the name of Jesus Christ of Nazareth rise up and walk" (v. 6). Peter was expectant. The man was expectant. No wonder something happened.

Dare to be expectant with yourself!

Too many of us have fallen into negative patterns of thinking about ourselves, perhaps because we have tried before and did not get anywhere, or perhaps because we think meanly of ourselves. We may say, "I don't count for anything," or "I can't do that," or "You can't expect me to measure up to that." Because there is no real anticipation in our own minds with regard to ourselves, we live at a low level.

Some have an expectancy level of zero for themselves. They just idle and drift—putty personalities, making no demands upon themselves. Others have a 50 percent level of expectancy for themselves. They get some things done. Some amount of hope, combined with a measure of discipline, keeps them from being totally soft with themselves.

Terribly few of us have an expectancy factor of 100 percent. We know too little of what John Wanamaker, the famous Philadelphia Christian merchant, meant when he said, "The most important lesson I have learned is that I have the least trouble with myself when I am giving myself to a worthwhile cause."

Dare to be expectant with others!

Peter was. He wanted to create in that beggar the feeling that there was someone who believed a new and wonderful thing could happen in his life.

Jesus was like that. Go back to the first chapter of the Gospel of John, verse 42. There was a fisherman in Galilee whose name was Peter. Jesus looked at him and said, "Thou art Simon the son of Jona: thou shalt be called Cephas"; and then John adds, "Which is by interpretation, A stone." He wasn't a man of rock at that moment—far from it. He was weak, vacillating, impulsive, high-tempered; Jesus knew it all. "Thou art" gives us the *realism* of

Jesus; "thou shalt be" gives us the *optimism* of Jesus. We need both. Even when Peter denied Him, our Lord did not lose faith. He said to him, "I have prayed for thee, that thy faith fail not" (Luke 22:32).

The trouble with some of us (I am surprised to find this even among Christians) is that we are so quick to write people off. "You can't do anything for him—he's impossible." So we put a label on him that says, "So far as I'm concerned, he's hopeless. I've given up on him."

May I say in deep seriousness, you can damn people into the nethermost hell by not having any confidence in their future. On the other hand, you can help God lift them to the highest heaven by believing they are worth saving, that they can be lifted out of the depths, that they can be put on the rails again and made useful members of the Church of the living God.

One of the greatest preachers of the English-speaking world was a so-called black sheep in his family. They gave him the feeling that he was hopeless. But one night in the wee hours, an aunt of his, guiding his unsteady feet to his room, said to him, "John, I have faith in you." She had breathed the magic word of positive expectancy that he so desperately needed. It was the turning point in his life.

Finally, *dare to be expectant with Christ!*

How could Peter say expectantly to the lame man, "Look on us"? Mind you, he had immediately to disillusion the poor fellow about one thing. He said, "Silver and gold have I none." What a letdown! Then the lift up: "But such as I have give I thee: In the name of Jesus Christ of Nazareth rise up and walk" (Acts 3:6). Ah, there's Peter's ultimate confidence. In "the name of Jesus Christ," the mighty Lord, he found the key to his real expectancy.

Years ago there was a little ditty from a Broadway musical comedy titled "How Can I Be What I Ain't?" It was sung by a rather unbeautiful character who yielded to one temptation after another and then regaled the crowd with this song.

Will it be any surprise to you to be told that this is a biblical question? Not in sordid jest, however, but rather in deep conflict and agony of spirit, the apostle Paul at one stage of his experience cries out, "What I would, that do I not; but what I hate, that do I. If then I do that which I would not . . . it is no more I that do it, but sin that dwelleth in me. . . . I find then a law, that, when I would do good, evil is present with me. . . . O wretched man that I am! who shall deliver me from the body of this death?" (Rom. 7:15-17, 21, 24).

But Paul does not stop there. He goes on to say triumphantly, "I thank God through Jesus Christ our Lord. . . . There is therefore now no condemnation to them which are in Christ Jesus, who walk not after the flesh, but after the Spirit. . . . For what the law could not do, in that it was weak through the flesh, God sending his own Son in the likeness of sinful flesh, and for sin, condemned sin in the flesh: that the righteousness of the law might be fulfilled in us, who walk not after the flesh, but after the Spirit" (v. 25; 8:1, 3-4).

"How can I be what I ain't?" I can't be until I dare to be expectant, looking to Jesus Christ, the crucified and risen Savior, who through His Holy Spirit can make me what I am not at this moment. I am not truthful; He can make me truthful. I am not pure; He can make me pure. I am not just and fair; He can make me right in my dealings with people. I am not loving and forgiving and gracious; He can make me tender and compassionate and kinder and forgiving. I can be what I ought to be if in Christ's presence I will dare to be expectant.

Part **III**

Bold Responses

15

THE PURE IN HEART

A Sermon Classic

TEXT: *Blessed are the pure in heart: for they shall see God* (Matt. 5:8).

THE RECURRENT NOTE IN THAT "HEAVENLY OCTAVE" that we know as the Beatitudes is the word "blessed." In the Phillips translation "blessed" is dropped, and "happy" is put in its place.

Whether the change is for the better or the worse is not easy to say. To say "happy" brightens up the translation, but it also thins it out. Everybody wants to be happy, but the happiness that "everybody" wants turns out often to be a disastrously selfish thing.

"Will the whole finance ministers and upholsterers and confectioners of modern Europe undertake in joint stock company to make one shoe-black happy?" asks Thomas Carlyle in that massive, explosive way of writing he had. And then, having flung out his challenge, well salted with sarcasm, he proceeds to set forth the reason why such a thing is impossible: "There is in man," he declares, "a higher than love of happiness; he can do without *happiness* and instead thereof find *blessedness.*"

There *is* a difference, isn't there?

The difference may be described in a variety of ways,

but one of them is this: Happiness is what a lot of unhappy people want by changing everything but themselves; blessedness is what nobody can have unless He is put right at the center.

It was to satisfy in people this "higher than love of happiness," of which Carlyle spoke truly, that Christ our Lord taught as He did, lived as He did, died as He did, and rose again as He did.

"Blessed are the pure in heart: for they shall see God." Only 11 words! But think where they take us! They are deep as the imperishable soul of man and woman and high as the infinite character of God. In thinking of them, let's start with something simple.

1. Our Lord believed in the *possibility* of a pure heart. Perhaps that statement strikes you as being a bit flat, pointless. It isn't. To feel its thrust, you need to remember the appalling things that Jesus knew—and reported—concerning the *impurity* of the human heart.

His inspection of the human interior resulted in something that reads like a sewer inspector's write-up: "From within, out of the heart of men, proceed evil thoughts, adulteries, fornications, murders, thefts, covetousness, wickedness, deceit, lasciviousness, an evil eye, blasphemy, pride, foolishness" (Mark 7:21-22).

Can *that* be so radically changed that the Savior, looking on the cleansed heart, calls it pure? If so, it's startling and glorious.

Eddying about this vital matter of heart purity are two views that oppose each other. Both of them have a hard time squaring things up with this God-man who utters himself so magnificently in the Sermon on the Mount.

On the one hand, *there are those who would tell us that the heart is by nature pure.* According to the latest bulletin, their number is not as large as it was back in Rousseau's day or even when our own American, John Dewey, was so popular at Columbia University.

Even the psychiatrists have joined the old-fashioned theologians in giving us a verdict on human nature that is anything but complimentary.

Still, there are those who optimistically hold that if you think you see any horns on human nature, you are quite mistaken. What is really there is a halo.

Over against this romantic view of the natural human heart is the gloomy belief not only that the heart is corrupt, but that *its corruption is in the last analysis incurable at any level or stage of experience this side of the grave.*

Here, surprisingly enough, some of our hoary creeds and catechisms speak with a despair that is difficult to reconcile with the great "emancipation" passages of the New Testament.

Thus a well-known catechism informs us that "no man, even by the aid of divine grace, can avoid sinning, but daily sins in thought, word, and deed."

If the framers of the catechism meant to point out that the saints, even at their holy best, are creatures of imperfection alongside the absolutely perfect God, then more felicitous words might have been chosen to express this thought.

Let's face it: If in one breath we tell the man or woman on the street that Jesus Christ came to "save his people from their sins" (Matt. 1:21), that through Him it is proposed that we should "serve him without fear, in holiness and righteousness before him, all the days of our life" (Luke 1:74-75), and in the next breath declare in solemn catechetical language that "no man, even by the aid of divine grace, can avoid sinning, but daily sins in thought, word, and deed," is not that man or woman on the street entitled to look at us with bewildered eye and charge us with contradiction and inconsistency? Would he or she not, in fact, be justified in telling us that, if the individual must live in daily sin of thought, word, and deed, the "salvation" that Jesus Christ offers looks far more like a gigantic failure than it does like a magnificent success?

This we cannot allow! Paul's impassioned words leap out to challenge any and every attempt, ancient, medieval, or modern, to make Christianity a device for coming to terms with sin: "Shall we continue in sin, that grace may abound? God forbid. How shall we, that are dead to sin, live any longer therein?" (Rom. 6:1-2).

"Blessed are the pure in heart: for they shall see God." Our Lord and His apostle are not at odds; they are in agreement.

Will you too agree? The Savior, knowing the worst about us, believes in the possibility of the best—nothing less than the possibility of a pure heart.

2. Take a still more searching and startling fact: our Lord reveals the *actuality* of a pure heart. "Blessed *are* the pure in heart" (emphasis added). The possible becomes the actual, the ideal the real.

Let's attempt something in the way of definition. What do we mean by a pure heart?

Two things we emphatically do *not* mean. We do not mean a heart *incapable of sin*. It is no "sinless perfection," in that sense, that we have in mind. Our capacity for wrong choices, for disobedience, for failures, for lapses from fellowship with God remain with us to the end.

A second negative: we do not mean a heart that is *exempt from temptation*. Faced with the necessity of keeping the body under, beset by all sorts of evil allurements in a spiritually uncongenial environment, assaulted by the devil in ways both daring and deceitful, the most deeply cleansed soul in all the wide ranges of the kingdom of God will have its conflicts and testings.

What, then, *do* we mean by a pure heart? The question persists.

I turn to John Peter Lange, the distinguished German commentator, and hear him say, "Purity of heart consists in that steady direction of the soul toward the divine life which excludes every other object from the homage of the heart."

I turn to a famous old Puritan—Thomas Manton—and I read, with due allowance for the stiffness of the older literary style: "Just as to sanctify signifieth to consecrate or dedicate to God, so it signifieth both the fixed inclination or the disposition of the soul towards God as our highest Lord and chief good, and accordingly a resignation of our souls to God, to live in the love of His blessed majesty and a thankful obedience to Him. More distinctly . . . it implieth a bent, a tendency, or fixed inclination towards God, which is habitual sanctification."

I turn to John Wesley, and I hear him say in a letter to a correspondent, "You never learned, either from my conversation or preaching or writings, that 'holiness consisted in a flow of joy.' I constantly told you quite the contrary: I told you it was love; the love of God and our neighbor; the image of God stamped on the heart; the life of God in the soul of man; the mind that was in Christ, enabling us to walk as Christ also walked."

I turn to George Arthur Buttrick, a contemporary Presbyterian, and I watch him solemnly write it down, in comment on Matt. 5:8, that "purity of heart" is a phrase in which "two meanings are perhaps dominant—rightness of mind and singleness of motive."

Or, remembering that often the poet gets closer to the heart of living realities than theologian or commentator, I turn to my hymnbook and read,

> O for a heart to praise my God,
> A heart from sin set free,
> A heart that always feels Thy blood,
> So freely shed for me.

A heart resigned, submissive, meek,
  My great Redeemer's throne,
Where only Christ is heard to speak,
  Where Jesus reigns alone.

O for a lowly, contrite heart,
  Believing, true, and clean,
Which neither life nor death can part
  From Him that dwells within.

—Charles Wesley

Finally, to climax it all, I turn to my Bible and read, "Now being made free from sin, and become servants to God, ye have your fruit unto holiness, and the end everlasting life" (Rom. 6:22). And similarly: "Now the end of the commandment is charity out of a pure heart, and of a good conscience, and of faith unfeigned" (1 Tim. 1:5).

A pure heart! What a really splendid thing! Motives laid open to the cleansing of God! The false ego consumed in the perpetual fires of the Holy Ghost and the real self offered up in a living flame of uttermost devotion to Christ!

This, says our Redeemer-Lord, is no mirage to mock a panting trekker on the desert. This is no flossy idealism far removed from the drab realities of everyday living. This is at once Christ's demand and Christ's offer. This is reality waiting to be taken!

3. Observe one thing more: Jesus declares the *felicity* of the pure heart. His words hold immensity within the compass of four monosyllables: "They shall see God."

What does that mean? More than any preacher's words can ever tell you!

But if their full significance is beyond us, shall we on that account run away from them? No.

If my eyes cannot take in the whole world of sunlight, shall I say they are useless? Sanity forbids. The light that does fall upon them—a fraction of the whole—is nevertheless the *real* thing.

When the father of the late M. S. Rice, distinguished Detroit pastor, was dying, he rallied his fast failing strength, lifted his tired head from the pillow, and as his mortal eyes dimmed in death, he murmured with soft exultation, "The vision! The vision!"

And his preacher-son, relating the incident, made this striking comment: "His soul could outsee his eyes."

That is the kind of vision about which we are now to think—not the hallucination of a madcap, not the conjured-up fantasies of a crystal gazer, not the unsubstantial images of trance or dream, but the penetrating insights and convictions of the man whose cleansed soul had been opened to God. The pure in heart will make all proper use of the eyes that are set in their heads, but they will never stop at that. Eyes for the world of the invisibles and the Kingdom of the eternals—that's what they have now! For theirs is the soul that can "outsee" the eyes. Theirs is the vision splendid!

For one thing, the pure in heart shall see God in *nature*. To Jesus the round earth and the common air and the star-strewn skies were full of the presence and power of the Father Almighty. His intimate nearness, Jesus was sure, could be mediated to the seeing soul by such easily overlooked things as a death-struck sparrow or a wayside flower.

In the first chapter of Romans the apostle Paul has a notable passage in which he indicts the pagan world on the ground that, although they have not had the light of Christ, they have glaringly and grossly failed to walk in the light that breaks through and shines from God's works.

"Look at the signs of God that you *do* have!" cries Paul to the non-Christian world. "You don't have a Cross on a hill called Calvary, but you do have the created world as the visible sign of an invisible Creator."

It is pride that blinds people. It is self-preoccupation that keeps them from seeing God at work in His world.

What incredible blindness it is that sends a man or woman reeling home at dawn after a night of carousal, blinking in drunken stupor at the gleaming splendors of a sunrise!

What strange myopia it is that causes even a Ph.D. to stare through microscope or telescope, discerning everything but the ultimately meaningful reality, seeing no faint signature of Deity, plucking nothing but scientific "blackberries."

> *Earth's crammed with heaven,*
> *And every common bush afire with God;*
> *But only he who sees takes off his shoes —*
> *The rest sit round it and pluck blackberries.*
>
> —Elizabeth Barrett Browning

It is different with the individual who has the pure heart. With vibrant voice and worshipful spirit, because with seeing eye, he or she joins with the ancient psalmist in crying, "The heavens declare the glory of God; and the firmament sheweth his handywork. Day unto day uttereth speech, and night unto night sheweth knowledge" (19:1-2).

Another poet has put the same fine appreciations in the form of a protest:

> *"No God! no God!" The simplest flower*
> *That on the wild is found,*
> *Shrieks as it drinks its cup of dew,*
> *And trembles at the sound.*
>
> *"No God," astonished Echo cries*
> *From out her cavern hoar:*
> *And every wandering bird that flies*
> *Reproves the Atheist lore.*
>
> *The solemn forest lifts its head*
> *The Almighty to proclaim;*
> *The brooklet on its crystal urn*
> *Doth leap to grave His name.*

High swells the deep and vengeful sea
Along its billowy track;
And red Vesuvius opes his mouth
To hurl the falsehood back.

"No God!" With indignation high
The fervent sun is stirred,
And the pale moon grows paler still,
At such impious word.

And from their burning thrones
The stars look down with angry eyes
That thus a worm of dust should mock
Eternal Majesty.

—Lydia H. Sigourney

"Oh," says someone, with a scornful tone, "all this talk about beholding God in nature is nonsense to me! What is the story of nature but an 'idiot's tale, full of sound and fury'? I can't see anything else."

Well, don't you wish you *could?* That was Turner's memorable reply to the lady who once told him that she never saw any actual sunsets that looked like those he painted.

"Don't you wish you could?"

Don't you wish that they would become so many mystic lenses through which you could sight the majestic figure and attract the moving form of Him who "hath measured the waters in the hollow of his hand, and meted out heaven with the span, and comprehended the dust of the earth in a measure, and weighed the mountains in scales, and the hills in a balance" (Isa. 40:12)?

If you do, let me point you to a poet's window through which you may see the secret:

I could see God tonight,
If my heart were right.
If all the rubbish of my soul
Were cleared away,

My being whole,
My breast would thrill in glad surprise
At all the wonder in my eyes.

If my heart were right,
I could see God tonight!
And in the radiance of His face
I'd flame with light and fill this place
With beauty and the world would know
The face of God down here below —
Tonight!
If only my dull heart were right!

The pure in heart, let me further suggest, see God in *events*. Some of you will have heard of the late Commissioner Samuel Logan Brengle, that saintly and winsome leader in the Salvation Army. Years ago, while participating in an open-air meeting, he was struck a brutal blow on the head by a brickbat flung from the hand of some ruffian. He was hurried to the hospital. For weeks he was confined to his bed.

While convalescing, he dictated from time to time a number of articles on what it means for Christians to live the life of the cleansed and the conquering. These articles appeared in the *War Cry* and were scattered far and near to the blessing of many. Finally he was discharged from the hospital and permitted to go home. He had not been in the house long when he made what struck him as an odd discovery. He found over the fireplace a piece of brick. On it was pasted a strip of paper inscribed with a verse of Scripture.

What had happened? Mrs. Brengle had saved the ugly missile that had struck him down and held him so long in the clutches of pain and over it had written the words of Joseph to his brethren after their father's death: "But as for you, ye thought evil against me; but God meant it unto good" (Gen. 50:20). Even then, after only a few weeks, Mrs. Brengle realized that his accident was somehow more than an accident—it was an arrangement by which something immeasurably fine and fruitful would come from his tested soul.

I remember vividly the first time he told this story to me. After referring to the series of articles in the *War Cry* later taking the form of a book titled *Helps to Holiness*, in which form they went winging and singing and preaching their way around the world, he laid his hand on my knee and, with a charming smile lighting up his saintly face, said, "So you see, if it had not been for the little *brick*, there would have been no little *book!*"

Do I say that it is *always* easy to see God in the events of our lives? I hope I know better than to say a thing so foolish as that. There are times when we seem to be denied even the slightest measure of understanding of the mystery of His providences.

Still, even at such times, the pure in heart have a quiet clairvoyance: by sheer, undaunted faith they see—God! They *trust* Him even where they cannot *trace* Him.

And then, taking the far look, let us try to realize that the pure in heart shall one day see God in *glory.*

"Now we see through a glass, darkly," Paul reminded the Corinthians; "but then face to face" (1 Cor. 13:12).

There is a perfected vision of God that lies beyond these mortal scenes and beyond the range of all vision of which even the children of God are now capable.

Let's try to trace out a thought or two on this. In John 1:18 we are told, "No man hath seen God at any time." That is to say, God, being a spirit, cannot report himself to any man's physical sense of sight. Pure spirit is beyond the reach of the natural eye.

If God is to reveal himself to His human creatures, He must accommodate himself to the creature's limitations. He must mediate His presence by some instrumentality that is reportable to the organ of sight.

This, as we know, is precisely what He did in Jesus of Nazareth, who in the mystery of His person was at once the Son of Mary and the Son of God. Hence in the verse that declares that "no man hath seen God at any time," we read, "The only begotten Son, which is in the bosom of the Father, he hath declared him" (John 1:18). We read also, "The Word was made flesh, and dwelt among us" (v. 14).

But mark this: When the Son of God, who was God from all eternity, became the Son of Man, the union of the human nature and the divine nature in the person of Jesus was not a temporary mystery—it was forever.

True, our Lord experienced a physical death in His crucifixion. Equally true is it that He mastered death, transcended death, overcame death, and arose in possession of a body that retained a definite link with the body that was laid in the tomb but which, nevertheless, Paul describes as a "spiritual body" (1 Cor. 15:44).

It was a body whose properties and powers are beyond our present comprehension. Still, whatever its exact nature, it continues to provide in some mysterious way a glorious embodiment for God himself. So true is this that the Holy Spirit, through the apostle John, has left us the assurance: "Beloved, now are we the sons of God, and it doth not yet appear what we shall be: but we know that, when he shall appear, we shall be like him; for *we shall see him as he is. And every man that hath this hope in him purifieth himself, even as he is pure*" (1 John 3:2-3, emphasis added).

The present purity and the future prospect are linked!

It is midsummer in Australia. In one of the rooms of a vine-clad cottage a Christian minister is dying. American evangelists Chapman and Alexander have slipped into the room. They are there by special request. Mr. Alexander is the first to reach the patient's couch. Following the moment of greetings, Mr. Alexander asks tenderly, "Can you sing?"

There is a pathetic wistfulness in the answer: "Oh, I wish you could have heard me sing when I had my voice!"

Mr. Alexander asks him if he has a song that he would like to hear sung.

As the pale face lights up, he answers, "Yes, do sing 'The Glory Song.'"

When Alexander has finished, the dying servant of Christ offers to sing something that has been dear to him for a long time. It is this:

> On the jasper threshold standing,
> Like a pilgrim safely landing,
> See the strange bright scenes expanding.
> This is heaven at last!

Dr. Chapman said later that, although he had heard 15,000 people joined in the singing of "The Glory Song" in Melbourne, he thought he had never heard anything so really heavenly as the music that came from the lips of this saintly minister.

After a momentary pause for the husbanding of such meager strength as he has left, he goes on through another stanza:

> Christ himself the living Splendor,
> Christ, the Sunlight mild and tender,
> Praises to the Lamb I'll render.
> This is heaven at last!

That is the shining terminus of the pilgrim's road!

Meanwhile, what about the pilgrim's own state? He or she hears the Savior say, "Blessed *are* the pure in heart." Nevertheless, like Thomas Cook, he or she is aware that "pride, envy, unbelief, self-will, and other forms of heart-sin" are there—mischievous disturbers of the inner peace.

What to do? How can he or she know the *reality* and live in the *release* of a pure heart?

Many years ago E. Stanley Jones wrote a book on the Holy Spirit in the life of the Christian. In the final chapter he suggested that the really healthy, holy Christian life is the outcome of falling deeply and utterly in love with Christ. And how? To which he replies, "How do we fall in love with anyone?"

Answering his own query, he deals with four steps: (1) a drawing near, (2) self-surrender, (3) trust, and (4) continuous adjustment.

Will you *draw near?* So near that you begin to see how stupidly trivial or wickedly inappropriate is everything outside of Christlikeness? So near that you seek nothing outside of Him—not even your holiness?

Will you make the total *self-surrender?* "Yield yourselves unto God, as those that are alive from the dead" (Rom. 6:13). Remember that self *as personality* is not destroyed; it is displaced. If this means being stung with the jibe that you are "eccentric," don't redden with anger—just radiate quiet joy. For to be "eccentric" means to be off center. And as long as we keep self-centered, we are off-centered. The throne within is not meant for self—that's tyranny by a petty dictator; it is meant for Christ—that's government by a benevolent Monarch!

Will you *trust?* The same Thomas Cook, deep in the throes of longing for inward adequacy and order, gained an insight that led him through the gate of victory: "I had received justification by faith, but was seeking sanctification by works."

To spell it out a bit, this is what happened: he asked some friends to join him in prayer that the secret of a pure heart might become his. While they were praying, 1 John 1:7 was brought home to him with, as he put it, "such power as I had never felt before"—"If we walk in the light, as he is in the light, we have fellowship one with another, and the blood of Jesus Christ his Son cleanseth us from all sin."

"I then saw," he testifies, "that the passage was not so much a promise as a plain declaration. If I walked in the light, the full cleansing from sin was my heritage, and all I had to do was immediately claim it. Without a moment's hesitation I did so."

Trust, you see. Not a shallow "Oh, yes, I believe!" but a deep and obedient commitment to His absolute Lordship.

And then—*continuous adjustment.* The wedding ceremony ("I pronounce that they are husband and wife together") is the work of a moment, but marriage is the task of a lifetime. And as any married person must confess, it is a task in *adjustment*.

So with the life of the pure in heart—adjusting to the unfolding of God's will! Adjusting to the thrust and darting of temptation! Adjusting to the painful evidences of immaturity that confront you even after the most crucial and significant realization of Christ's sanctifying Lordship! Adjusting to the fact that a pure heart is never like a cavity out of which a bad tooth has been extracted, but always like your body when a fever has left you. The fever is *gone*, but the danger of reinfection is never entirely removed. If the health tone is kept high, the germs may attack, but they can't infect.

It is not otherwise with the pure in heart; only as they continue in vital union with the cleansing Savior through a moment-by-moment faith and obedience can they *live* and *love* and *serve* as those in whom God has "begun a good work" and will "perform it until the day of Jesus Christ" (Phil. 1:6).

> *Not I, but Christ, my every need supplying;*
> *Not I, but Christ, my strength and health to be;*
> *Christ, only Christ, for body, soul, and spirit;*
> *Christ, only Christ, live then Thy life in me.*
> —Mrs. A. A. Whiddington

Who now will let Christ lead you from the *possibility* to the *actuality* and on to the *felicity* of the pure in heart?

16

THE ALLURE OF
THE HOLY

"WORSHIP THE LORD IN THE BEAUTY OF HOLINESS," exclaims
the psalmist (29:2).

The lengthening years deepen my conviction that,
when all is said and done, there is something beautiful
about Christian holiness. It is the beauty of God. It is the
liveliness of Christ.

If this conviction is well-founded, as I believe it is, then
it compels me to say that much that passes for holiness—
much that is grim and grumbly, much that is sour and censorious, much that is narrowly legalistic and pharisaically
repressive—has to be ruled out as somehow counterfeit.

A woman once engaged me in conversation, saying she
was concerned because in wide areas of the church life of
today there is so little said or felt concerning the glowing
biblical theme of holiness. I joined her in deploring this.
But what I missed in her was the quiet radiance of Jesus.
She was gloomy, strained, negative.

I listened to a Holiness evangelist denouncing mod-
ernism. Turning up the heat for his final eruption of indignation, he quoted an eminent modernist and vigorously
proclaimed, "If that man is not going to hell, there's no use
to have a hell!" Even if eternity proves the evangelist to
have been right, the question may still be asked: Was

Christian holiness commended to anyone by a judgment so harshly expressed? I for one believe that when Jesus uttered the shattering austerities of Matt. 23, there was tenderness in His voice because there was pathos in His heart.

At the close of a Sunday morning service, when nearly everyone had left the church building, a lady said to me, "Do you have a few moments you could give to a frustrated pastor's wife who says her prayers one minute and screams at her children the next minute?"

Why is there something incongruous about behavior such as this?

One possible answer is: it just isn't beautiful.

More than 30 times in the Greek New Testament there appears a word that is usually translated "good," "goodness," or "well." For example, "Let us not be weary in well doing: for in due season we shall reap, if we faint not" (Gal. 6:9). The word may, however, be rendered "fair" or "beautiful." Holy living is beautiful living. Purity that is negative, self-conscious, weird, and denunciatory is like lilies that have begun to rot: ill smelling.

Those who philosophize about beauty are not always agreed in its essential characteristics. Yet some qualities have been given a high rating in any definition of beauty.

For example—truthfulness. Perhaps today the better word would be *reality.* Pretense and sham are beauty spoilers. The insight of David was sound when he told God: "Thou desirest truth in the inward parts" (Ps. 51:6).

In beauty there is, too, a quality that the experts often call richness. It is the artistic plus. It is curiously not precisely the same as excess, for that comes under the head of the superfluous, the extravagant; it is the fullness that excels without being excessive. A fussy straining after piety is not beautiful. It is pathetic. Christian holiness, on the other hand, is an overflow of the indwelling Christ. It has no need to be wheezily pumped up. It is artesian.

The beauty analysts ask for another thing if beauty is to be authentic: they insist on the quality of proportion. The element of balance cannot be ignored, they say. Jesus must have felt the ugly imbalance of the Pharisees, who went about punctiliously tithing little bits and pieces of "mint and anise and cummin" while neglecting such plain, obvious responsibilities as "judgment, mercy, and faith" (Matt. 23:23).

This quality of proportion, by which the "beauty of holiness" may be judged, wears many lovely faces: the ability to disagree without being disagreeable, the gift of a faithful witness to truth combined with respect for minds other than one's own, the art of abstaining without being proud of the abstention or censorious toward those who fail to abstain, the discipline of maintaining scruples in a healthy conscience without the neuroticism of manufacturing scruples over nonexistent or secondary issues.

Blessed are the balanced! A man of God was asked how he felt about leaving a church he had served for years. His quaint and picturesque answer: "There's a tear in one eye and a twinkle in the other!" If it had been either "all tears" or "all twinkle," it would have been abnormal. What prevailed was not eccentricity or morbidity, but wholesome balance. The balance of a man of God through whom shone "the beauty of holiness" (Ps. 29:2).

Whence comes this beauty—and how?

It comes from Christ. "Let the beauty of Jesus be seen in me!" (Albert Orsborn)

We can say, I think, that the secret is twofold: a radical cleansing and a regular contemplation. "Create in me a clean heart" (Ps. 51:10)—something deeply decisive! "We all, with unveiled face, beholding the glory of the Lord, are being changed into his likeness from one degree of glory to another" (2 Cor. 3:18, RSV)—something progressively transfiguring!

Neither without the other is enough. Together they insure *the allure of the holy.*

17

DON'T USE PRAYER— PRAY!

LIN YÜ-T'ANG, A BRILLIANT CHINESE PHILOSOPHER and author, left us an account of how he was driven away from faith in Christianity. What alienated him, he declared, was the ineffectual prayer of one of his relatives who asked God for fine weather for a funeral. As it turned out, the weather was bad.

Is this the way we prove or disprove prayer? If so, we are in difficulties. After all, God is not a sort of cosmic bellhop, running up and down the corridors of our world and delivering desirable kinds of weather to each praying man's door.

Take another example of muddleheadedness in prayer. A famous actress was being interviewed by a reporter for a New York newspaper. She said among other things that she believed in prayer. The reporter, however, made a revealing comment about her prayerfulness. Said he, "She's not timid about asking for help, either. For around her neck, on a thin gold chain, there are three religious symbols—the cross, the miraculous medal, and the Jewish Star of David!"

How interesting! Here is a point of view that seems to say, "Let's play the field—Protestant, Roman Catholic, Jewish—in the hope of getting everything out of God that we can!" Here, in fact, is a kind of utilitarian shrewdness that eats the heart out of prayer.

Or again, an article I saw was titled "How the Psychologist Uses Prayer." That word "uses" suggests how we can cheapen prayer into a selfish device after the fashion of put a dime in the slot and out comes the package you want!

This is a view of prayer that takes too little notice of its deeper meanings, is too little concerned about the linking of the life with God as the One in whose very nature of love and holiness we are to proceed with the business of living.

Prayer that is genuinely Christian is a way of *surrendering*. God gives himself as well as His gifts to those who give themselves to Him. Picking up a little booklet on prayer, I was struck with the very first sentence: "We do not start with prayer, but with God." That puts the emphasis where it belongs—not on ourselves, not on things, but on God.

"For he that cometh to God," says the writer to the Hebrews, "must believe that he is, and that he is a rewarder of them that diligently seek him" (11:6)—not His blessings, not His gifts, but Him: His mind, His heart, His purpose.

Prayer is not barging into the King's audience room with a hot and hasty request. Prayer is, in the first instance, humbly, consciously, freshly relating one's life and being to God—to all of God whom we see revealed in Jesus Christ our Lord.

Again, prayer is a way of *strengthening*. When the early Christians described in Acts 4 were in trouble with the hostile authorities, their prayer was "And now, Lord, behold their threatenings: and grant unto thy servants, that with all boldness they may speak thy word" (v. 29). Notably absent was a prayer for safety. Notably present was a prayer for courage. That the prayer was impressively answered is indicated in the narrative: "With great power gave the apostles witness of the resurrection of the Lord Jesus" (v. 33).

All of us humans lean on something for strength. What is tragic is to find that so many of us lean on puny props and fickle forces when we might lean, through prayer, on the utterly dependable power of the Spirit of God.

Prayer, besides being a way of *surrendering* and a way of *strengthening*, is a way of *seeing*.

Vision and understanding at the deeper levels of life—what desperate need we have for just these! "No man," said Emerson, "ever prayed without learning something." I believe that is true, provided it be really prayer, real communion with God and not the pious mouthing of empty phrases.

How often do we acknowledge that we are prone to let intolerance, passion, and prejudice rule our judgments and color our memories? Do we realize that quick guesses and hasty surmises and garbled information, together with too much pride of private opinion, can fog our outlook on people and situations? Do we accordingly look upon prayer as a potent means by which the Spirit of God breaks through these barriers and gives us insight into ourselves and others?

There is a poem I've had in my file for a long time, one verse of which goes:

> *I never can hide myself from me;*
> *I see what others may never see.*
> *I know what others may never know.*
> *I never can fool myself, and so,*
> *Whatever happens, I want to be*
> *Self-respecting and conscience-free.*

But is the poet right? Is it true and "I never can fool myself"? That is exactly the trouble with many of us. We can, and we do, fool ourselves.

It is not too much to say that real prayer probes deeper within us than any exercise in which we can engage. George Arthur Buttrick in his monumental book on prayer quotes Dwight L. Moody, who once wrote in a man's Bible,

"This Book will keep you from your sins, or your sins will keep you from this Book."

"Thus we might say," added Buttrick, "sincere prayer will keep you from self-deception, or self-deception will keep you from your prayers."

Don't use prayer—really pray! God is not a gadget, and prayer is not a tool. Prayer is an aliveness between ourselves and Him in which, when we want Him and His way more than all else, anything can happen.

18

THE CALL IS FOR HOLY WORLDLINESS

"NONSENSE," SOMEONE WILL BE INSTANTLY TEMPTED TO SAY upon hearing the term "holy worldliness." "There is no such thing. All worldliness is unholy."

That there is an unholy worldliness—a worldliness that is spiritually deadening and finally damning—is too clear a teaching of the New Testament to leave room for debate. Quickly to mind comes Jesus' solemn query: "For what is a man profited, if he shall gain the whole world, and lose his own soul?" (Matt. 16:26). Equally easy to recall is Paul's admonition to the Christians at Rome: "Be not conformed to this world" (12:2). Even more explicit is the warning that John wrote to the believers: "Love not the world, neither the things that are in the world. If any man love the world, the love of the Father is not in him. For all that is in the world, the lust of the flesh, the lust of the eyes, and the pride of life, is not of the Father, but is of the world" (1 John 2:15-16).

Here is worldliness with blight: it *damages, defiles, destroys.* And its essence is not found in specific forms of behavior. Its essence lies in an attitude that rates the temporal above the eternal, the material above the spiritual.

From this worldliness we need to be set free, as indeed we can be in the measure in which we offer ourselves to the sanctifying Lordship of Christ over all our attitudes and aims.

Meanwhile, let's face it: we have not said it all when we say that Christians are to be set free from the world and are required to bear witness against the cunning and corrosive way in which worldliness destroys the faith, vision, and dedication that should mark the redeemed life.

Listen to Jesus: "I pray not that thou shouldest take them out of the world, but that thou shouldest keep them from the evil. . . . As thou hast sent me into the world, even so have I also sent them into the world" (John 17:15, 18).

Listen again to John: "As he is, so are we in this world" (1 John 4:17).

Let me put it this way: if, on the one hand, there is an unholy worldliness in relation to which the Christian needs to understand the meaning of separation, there is, on the other hand, a holy worldliness in relation to which the Christian needs to understand the meaning of identification. Yet the crucial point of the matter is not completely stated in that sentence. It is important to see that each of the two positions—the separation and the identification—is involved in the other. And it is this *involvement* that too many people, in the attempt to be spiritually-minded, are trying to escape. Let me illustrate.

The wife of a Christian leader whom I know in Scotland tells of going to a weekend retreat arranged by the young people of a large and active Scottish congregation. These were really young adults who were either in the last stage of their education or in the professions. She learned that for their devotional use in the retreat—and indeed for the winter that lay ahead—they had chosen Thomas à Kempis's *Imitation of Christ*. Excellent, one might say! Yes, so far as it goes. But she made another discovery. She found that these young people, who took good religious doses of Thomas à Kempis in the "quiet hour," seemed to carry none of it over into the ordinary occasions of the day. Instead, at mealtimes and other times of conversation, their talk was largely about their jobs and why one was better than another—better, that is, in such things as pay, promotional prospects, vacations, and other fringe benefits.

Analyze this, and see what you have. Fifteen minutes—make it 30 if you wish—with Thomas à Kempis, where the stress is on *self-denial!* A fraction of the day in which you conduct yourself like a saint! The bulk of the day in which you conduct yourself under no profession of allegiance to Jesus Christ!

This is splitting life right down the middle. This is part of what is meant by being "double-minded." If table talk is to be about jobs, why not about the "Christianizing" of those jobs, how to make them witness for Christ, how to do better work, how to recover (for oneself and for others) the almost lost sense of the dignity of work, how to exert Christian influence (both on employers and employees) to create better relations between those who hire and those who are hired, how to cultivate, for their own sake, persons with whom we work in order that the friendship and confidence thus created may be used by the Spirit of God to bring them to faith in the same Savior who found and changed us?

Here, you see, is holy worldliness. Here is separation—at the level of the mind; here, at the same time, is identification at the level of Christian practice.

Why not? Christianity is the gospel of the Incarnation—the Word become flesh.

The "Word"—spiritual. The "flesh"—secular. Conflict? No.

What then? The Word above the flesh, to be sure. But the Word identifying itself with the flesh—redeeming it, hallowing it, utilizing it.

The call is for holy worldliness!

19

THE TONE OF THE BELL

ZECH. 14:20 SPEAKS OF BELLS bearing the inscription "HOLINESS UNTO THE LORD." It's a description that fires one's fancy, enriches one's imagination.

Also, it sets in motion some long thoughts! Bells do get cracked at times. The sound doesn't cease—the beauty of the tone does.

Here are some cracks in the bell that we who embrace biblical holiness would do well to avoid or, if they have already appeared, to repair:

1. Excessive self-consciousness. Self-conscious holiness is not attractive. It may fool some people, but not many. If Jesus had gone along with Satan's bid and had cast himself down from "a pinnacle of the temple" (Luke 4:9), thrill seekers might have been impressed, but the rest of us are eternally thankful He stayed in the wilderness and quietly fought it out.

A viper bit Paul and did him no harm. But far from Paul's mind was the staging of any stunt or the bringing forward of any proof. David danced before the ark. He didn't do it to gain attention. Attention was something that he as king didn't need. But have you noticed how easy it is for some of us to "perform" before the congregation? We claim it as "freedom" when perhaps we should have disclaimed it as "exhibitionism."

2. Needless argumentativeness. Christian holiness is seldom advanced by controversy; it is never advanced by controversy cankered with bitterness or puffed up with pride. Purity of heart and piety of life have always needed more witnesses than lawyers, more demonstrators than judge-advocates. A Calvinist with Canaan's fruit in his or her basket is more pleasing to God and convincing to people than an Arminian with Egypt's leeks on his or her breath.

3. Defensive competitiveness. When Pentecost came, we read of the "big fisherman:" "But Peter, standing up with the eleven . . ." (Acts 2:14). It wasn't always so. There had been times when the Eleven were not "with" one another but "against" one another. Jealousies split them. Rivalries divided them. Carnal competition tore them.

The peril is still with us. The fault has not disappeared from us—not wholly. Paying lip service to Pentecost is not enough. The flame of it must consume us. When it does, we are fused—not driven together, nor frozen together, but melted together.

Always, of course, there is the proneness to defend our competitiveness. "Excuses" are decked out with the deceptive colors of "reasons." "Opinions" are wreathed with the solemn halos of "convictions."

The one thing missing is—Calvary! Calvary—where the most refined bigotries are smashed! Calvary—where defending a point of view or promoting a organization is as nothing compared with the holy call to "shew forth the praises of him who hath called you out of darkness into his marvellous light" (1 Pet. 2:9).

Let's make it our aim to tune the bells of our lives so that, uncracked and unmistakably, they will chime, "HOLINESS UNTO THE LORD"!

20

GOD IN SHACKLES

"GOD HANGS THE EARTH UPON NOTHING, but He hangs destinies upon that invisible hinge named the human will. Deity can manage His worlds, but He asks your consent to help you manage your life." These arresting sentences are taken from a sermon once preached by Frederick Shannon of Chicago.

It is we who put shackles upon God. We cannot keep Him from managing the stars above us, but we can prevent Him from managing the soul within us. That was what ancient Israel did, according to the mournful 78th psalm.

In it we have a poem of disobedience, dishonor, and disgrace for Israel, and of disappointment and delay for God. Make certain soundings in the psalm, and this is what you come up with:

"They kept not the covenant of God, and refused to walk in his law" (v. 10).

"They believed not in God, and trusted not in his salvation" (v. 22).

"They did flatter him with their mouth, and they lied unto him with their tongues" (v. 36).

Then in verse 41 comes the statement that has caught my attention: "They turned back and tempted God, and limited the Holy One of Israel." Dr. Hull in his *Two Thou-*

sand Hours in the Psalms renders it, "They drew a circle around the Holy One."

It is possible, then—shockingly possible, I think we should say—to throw up barriers in the way of the Almighty. You and I can hinder Him in carrying out His large and lovely purpose for our lives.

Let me first of all raise the question, In what *areas* of life do we limit God—yes, even we Christians? Take the matter of God's *claims,* for example. Here is our week of seven days. The first day we call "the Lord's day." We draw a circle around it and shut God up within it. The other days are ours. They are open. They are at our disposal, whereas Sunday is at His disposal. Does it not occur to us that when we do that, we are limiting the Holy One of Israel?

Or we say of hymn singing and prayer, "This is God's business!" So we draw a circle around our devotional activities and discreetly enclose the Lord within it. But what about the rest of my activities—the job I have to perform, the business I have to conduct, the farm I have to operate? Does God want to be counted in on my worship and then counted out of my work? Not if He means business when He says, "And whatsoever ye do in word or deed, do all in the name of the Lord Jesus" (Col. 3:17).

In addition to limiting God in the area of His claims, do we not also limit Him in the sphere of His *power?* This indeed is clearly the main failure of Israel so far as the 78th psalm is concerned. In the 72 verses of the psalm is an easily discovered pattern: first, the recital of God's dealings with His people in various demonstrations of His strength and faithfulness; and second, the complaint of the psalmist over the fears and failures of the people.

"Look and see what God did," cries this distressed writer, "and then see with what folly and disobedience the people treated Him." When He had brought them through the Red Sea, why could they not trust Him for water in the wilderness? But no, they grew angry and panicky. "Where-fore," they complained to Moses, "is this that thou hast brought us up out of Egypt, to kill us and our children and our cattle with thirst?" (Exod. 17:3). If it wasn't water, it was food. If it wasn't food, it was the threat of their ene-mies. If it wasn't enemies, it was dissatisfaction with Moses' leadership. Thus they limited God's power.

Some of us are in danger of doing the very same thing. But Jesus is saying, "All power is given unto me in heaven and in earth" (Matt. 28:18), and to that He adds, "Give me thine heart."

Let me now raise with you a second question that grows out of our theme: By what *attitudes* do we circum-scribe God and hinder His free working in our lives?

For one thing, we do it by an attitude of *unwillingness to learn from the past.* This accusation is made sharply in one of the early verses of the psalm. "They forgot what he had done, and the miracles that he had shown them" (RSV), says verse 11. History is a tremendous teacher, but in most of us she finds listless and unwilling pupils. We need to learn the fine art of the psalmist, who cried, "Bless the LORD, O my soul, and forget not all his benefits" (103:2). It's forgetting that is fatal.

Unwillingness to learn from the past—and then a sec-ond attitude that shackles the Lord God: the attitude of *un-belief in His Word and power.* Let verses 21 and 22 tell their guilty story: "So a fire was kindled against Jacob, and anger also came up against Israel; because they believed not in God, and trusted not in his salvation." Unbelief puts a circle around God, limiting His power, denying His promises.

That is what it did for the Israelites. God's power brought them out of Egypt, but they put a circle around it and refused to believe that He could provide food when they needed it. The food was given, and they put a circle around that providence, refusing to believe that He could send them water in the desert. The water was supplied, and they put a circle around *that* deliverance, refusing to believe that He could defend them against their foes. And on it went, until the day came when the consequences of their unbelief moved in upon them in stark tragedy. "He gave his people over also unto the sword," says verse 62; "and was wroth with his inheritance."

We have a great God. He is not limited in himself, but He is limited in us. Where we are concerned—our guilts and our fears and our longings—He is free to work only as we give Him a chance.

21

I SHALL GO TO MY GRAVE

I AM NOT ILL—NOT MORBID, NOT DESPONDENT. To the best of my knowledge, I am not suffering from what some psychiatrists would call a "death wish."

On the other hand, I am not young. The 20th century and I have kept close company for many years. I have outlived all those senior men of God who helped to mold and mature me when I was a youthful preacher in the making. More than that, I have outlived many of my peers, respected and much-loved contemporaries.

So I speak in a mood neither callow nor melancholy.

Let me try to ring some bells that resonate with my strong and persistent convictions:

I shall go to my grave affirming that Jesus Christ is what I mean by absolute reality. Not the Church, which is less than eternal; not the Bible, which is instrumental rather than ultimate; but Jesus Christ, the Lord revealed.

I shall go to my grave convinced that the Church—the visible community of Christian faith and fellowship—needs to exhibit a unity that is perilously contradicted by the exclusive, self-defensive, and often warring divisions into which we have fractured and factioned ourselves. With time's passing I am less and less impressed by our attempts to justify this rabbit warren proliferation of our sects and subdivisions. Concurrently I am increasingly struck by the flimsiness and self-giving of our arguments for going on as we are.

I shall go to my grave declaring that the human condition of estrangement from God is so profound that it can never be put right except as He in mercy takes the initiative, as He has in Christ. At the Cross, the place of reconciliation has been found and founded once for all and for all who will kneel to accept.

I shall go to my grave persuaded that the rules and regulations for Christians, if used as means by which we pigeonhole our Christian comrades into "true" or "false," are legalistic devices for producing "cult" or "culture" Christianity instead of the beloved community of the New Testament.

I shall go to my grave firm in the feeling that one of the most frequent undetected sins of Christians is idolatry. Customs, tradition, forms, ideologies, organizations, institutions (including the state), precedents, structures, titles, clichés—in every one of them there is a potential idol. They arose, it well may be, out of historical necessity. We cling to them or kowtow to them or somehow perpetuate them out of lethargy, bigotry, stupidity, or vanity.

I shall go to my grave believing that the long years of controversial "pulling and hauling" over the personal gospel was a poignant miscalculation. There was myopia on both sides. Now, thank God, the signs point to clearer understanding.

I shall go to my grave with the conviction that theological tunnel vision has kept multitudes of Christians, both clergy and laity, from discovering the wealth of Christlikeness that is open to them on the pages of the New Testament. A holiness of motivating love, offered both as gift and as growth, has been missed by masses of Christians. They have missed it because of their preoccupation with two-nature theories, or "after all I'm only human" rationalizations, or mistaken exegesis ("Paul saw himself a bigger sinner at the end than at the beginning of his Christian life"), or justifiable fears of perfectionist excesses that they have witnessed or that history has recorded. We are wrong, I am persuaded, to set limits to what the grace of God can do in redeeming and refashioning the believing person.

I shall go to my grave asserting that nine-tenths of our either/ors are abstractions of the mind rather than reflections of reality. There *are* absolutes, and there *is* truth in situation ethics. There *is* subordination in family and other community life, and there *is* sexual equality. We *do* have a trustworthy Bible, and we *do* have a Bible whose authority is not derailed by a misspelled word or an erroneously translated term or an incorrect date.

I shall go to my grave believing that, side by side with my ardent expectation of the Second Advent, most of our "signs of the times" sermons and books are based on opportunism and a mistaken understanding of what the apocalyptic portions of Scripture are meant to teach us. These hot sermonic and literary outpourings tend, in the cases of many Christians, to distract from the "occupy till I come" (Luke 19:13) mandate for missions and social responsibility.

I shall go to my grave unshakable in the faith confession that, all appearances to the contrary, "Jesus is Lord."